"*Hanging Boots: From Guns to Garlands* is a book which you come across once in a lifetime. The real events of how militants from NE India transitioned into mainstream society...through meditation, yoga, peace talks and Gurudev's blessings... is worth a read. Vishnu Prakash writes with genuine heart and humor."

—***Saurav Somani***

Chartered Accountant; Author & Columnist for the Assam Tribune

"*Hanging Boots* demonstrates a real-life miracle, demonstrating how meditation and human values can quietly yet decisively change lives and, in doing so, change the world."

—***Dr. Khushraj Madnani,***

Faculty, Department of Computer Science, Indian Institute of Technology – Guwahati;

Former Postdoctoral Fellow, Max Planck Institute for Software Systems (2022–2025);

Former Postdoctoral Fellow, TU Delft, The Netherlands (2020–2022);

Ph.D. & M.Tech., IIT Bombay; B.Tech., NIT Surat

"*Hanging Boots* is a powerful kick to the soul. Vishnu's raw journey from the pitch to purpose is honest and profoundly motivating. Every educator and dreamer needs this on their shelf!"

—***Rupraj Dey,*** *M.Sc., B.Ed., M.A., PGDIPR*

Principal, Adarsha Vidyalaya, Dewan T.E.

"Vishnu writes with a rare sincerity that feels both intimate and universal. Every page is infused with sensitivity, devotion, and a quiet spiritual depth that gently touches the soul."

—Nishant P Pathak

VP, Deutsche Bank

"Vishnu has written each chapter so candidly that it tugs the string of devotion in every reader's heart."

—Dr. Arnab Bhattacharya, MBBS,

K. M. Medical College and Hospital, Mathura, Uttar Pradesh

HANGING BOOTS

FROM **GUNS** TO **GARLANDS**

VISHNU PRAKASH

गरुड

Published by
Garuda Prakashan Private Limited
Gurugram, Bharat

www.garudalife.in

First published in Bharat 2026

ISBN: 978-93-47691-76-8

Printed in Bharat

Disclaimer

This book is a reflection of my personal experiences and perspectives. The views and opinions expressed herein are solely my own, and I take full responsibility for all content presented. Any organizations, institutions, or individuals mentioned are not responsible for these views.

The intent of this work is not to cause harm, defame, or negatively impact any individual or group, whether mentioned directly or indirectly.

While every effort has been made to accurately represent real-life events and experiences, certain details—including timelines—may contain minor inaccuracies due to the limitations of memory and documentation.

Although this book references real people, associations, groups, and organizations, some names and identifying details have been changed to protect privacy and maintain sensitivity.

Hanging Boots Team with Gurudev

CONTENTS

Preface

I wrote this book to document a rare and quiet alchemy—the moment when the gears of war are brought to a halt by a vision that refuses to accept violence as inevitable. While my name appears on the cover, this is not my story. It is a chronicle of the extraordinary intervention of Gurudev Sri Sri Ravi Shankar in a conflict that had defied resolution for generations.

For many, Gurudev is synonymous with meditation and inner peace. But standing in the mud of Dima Hasao and sitting across from men who had spent their lives in the jungle, I witnessed a far deeper dimension of his work. He did not merely offer these men a way to quiet their minds; he offered a way to save their lives and their land. Where others saw an intractable insurgency, he saw a wound in India's Northeast that had been festering for over seventy years—and chose to address it not only as a spiritual teacher, but as a guardian of the nation's soul.

Gurudev's role went far beyond traditional diplomacy. He recognized that the solution to insurgency does not lie solely in the signing of agreements, but in the complete removal of the trust deficit between people and the state. He created a spiritual umbrella under which even the most hardened commanders felt safe enough to emerge from the shadows. This book explores how his vision speaks to the most complex and seemingly "secular" challenges facing a nation—demonstrating that when the heart is healed, politics follows.

What compelled me to write was the need to document Gurudev's tireless labor in the Northeast. I witnessed how his presence could systematically replace decades of fear with an overwhelming sense of belonging. My own journey—leaving behind a corporate career for the unpredictable terrain of Assam—was simply a response to that vision. I was a witness to the impossible becoming real because Gurudev chose to step in where many others had withdrawn.

This narrative is drawn from the front-row seat I occupied as an instrument of his work. It is built from personal journals, memories of high-stakes negotiations he guided, and transformative moments I was privileged to facilitate under his direction. These experiences are supplemented by direct testimony from former top leadership of the DNLA, official records, and first-hand documentation of the "cowshed celebrations," where Gurudev's message turned warriors into peacemakers.

Writing about a living conflict demands care, safety, and integrity. I have handled the stories of former cadres with sensitivity, ensuring their dignity and security is preserved. This book does not seek to sanitize the past—the violence that preceded this peace was real. But the success documented here stands as proof that no one is beyond the reach of transformation when a higher force intervenes.

The journey that follows mirrors the path Gurudev laid out—beginning with the psychological shift I call the *Death of Doubt* and moving toward the final, triumphant laying down of arms. Ultimately, this is a book about the power of a single vision to heal a nation. It is the story of how Gurudev reached into the darkness of the jungle and brought a forgotten people home.

Prologue

"We will not stop till the last gun is laid down in the region."
—Gurudev

The air inside Radha Kunj was unnervingly still for a room housing the leaders of the last active insurgent group in Assam. It was 9:45 p.m.—a time when the rest of the Bengaluru Ashram was settling into the rhythmic silence of night—but for the three men seated across from Gurudev, the world was still loud with the echoes of the jungle.

Mukteshwar Kemprai, advisor to the Dimasa National Liberation Army (DNLA), sat with a stillness that felt like a coiled spring. Beside him were Etika Diphusa, the group's president, and their commander-in-chief—men more accustomed to the humidity of the Myanmar border and the weight of a rifle than the scent of sandalwood and the soft glow of a spiritual sanctuary. Between them lay a memorandum. Its letterhead, marked by two crossed swords, was a stark intrusion of war into a house of peace.

Gurudev did not skim the document. He read it line by line, his finger tracing demands for a sovereign, independent Dimasa nation—a dream for which these men had spent decades hiding in the shadows, fearing no leopard or python, only the presence of other humans.

The silence that followed was heavy and unresolved. For years, the government had been a wall they could not scale;

the Intelligence Bureau, a shadow they could not shake. They were exhausted. Mukteshwar's eyes—usually sharp and diplomatic—were weary. Earlier that evening, he had told Vishnu that he was mentally spent, trapped in what he called a "mental sandwich," crushed between the suffering of cadres in the hills and the relentless pressure of investigating agencies.

Then Gurudev looked up.

His first question was not about politics, but about reality.

"Is there anyone among you who can actually lead such a nation?" he asked gently. "Run it, guide it, hold it?"

The room went cold. It was the one question no guerrilla warfare manual had prepared them for. Mukteshwar lowered his gaze to the floor. The commander-in-chief—a man who had once planned precise ambushes—stared at his own hands. The idea of a separate country, landlocked and isolated, suddenly felt like a heavy stone carried for no one.

"Why limit yourself to Dima Hasao?" Gurudev continued, his voice soft but unmistakably firm. "Why not think of Assam… and of India?"

The stakes were absolute. If the dialogue failed, they would return to the jungle—to camps where "special pig meat" and indigenous wine masked a brutal order, where young men were shot in the legs as punishment or fed local poisons for breaking organizational rules. But to stay meant surrendering more than weapons. It meant surrendering identity.

"We cannot surrender to the government," Mukteshwar whispered, the honesty of the statement cutting through the room. "But we can surrender to you, Gurudev. Will you be our interlocutor?"

In that single question lay the tension of the years to come—the shift from fear to hope, from the trust deficit of a war zone to the slow repair of a fractured community.

Gurudev nodded without hesitation. Reaching out, he gently pulled Etika's cheeks—a gesture at once playful and maternal. Something in the room softened. Decades of hardened resolve briefly gave way.

As they stepped into the cool Bengaluru night, the men were no longer rebels. They chased a departing car, shouting "Jai Gurudev" with a fervor that once belonged to a very different cause. The last gun had not yet been laid down, but the last doubt had begun to dissolve.

This transformation was no overnight miracle. It was forged over years—of walking a razor's edge in the Northeast, of corporate resignations, of a perfectionist who once submerged himself in an unclean river in Diphu just to prove that service was real.

Long before the peace accords were signed in New Delhi, the journey had begun with a single celebration in a newly built cowshed, where seventy-six men wept openly—having discovered a peace utterly unlike the violence they once believed in.

It all began with the Death of Doubt.

My Self...

I am peaceful and quiet,
I am the unchanging light.
The 'You' in 'me',
And the 'Me' in 'you'.

I rest in the Self—
This is my deepest wealth.
Always pure, ever present,
Beyond past, beyond future.

I know only this wish:
I am the bliss.

I Never Knew

I never knew
When or how

I was filled with love and light,
My life began to flow
Upward and right.

All I comprehend is
Your unfathomable presence,

Dropping all grievances,
Spreading the fragrance of love.

From being somebody to being nobody,
And from being nobody to everybody.

I never knew
When or how,

I am with the Divine,
Simply to smile
And shine.

Grace is Unconditional

The mind stands invincible,
while thoughts become innumerable.
I walk alone
through the silent zone,
cloaked in my own disguise
as moments drift together and fly.

Is this all mundane,
or is every step part of a sacred pain —
a churning meant to awaken?

O my Dear Divine,
I only seek to find:
Who am I?

Racing through
the quest of enquiry,
soothing silence
and experiencing Your permanent Presence,
Gurudev...

It is a mutual affair—
I sense it—
love is in the air.

Being Happy... Making Others Happy

Before this life completes,
Do something sweet—
That, truly, is a real treat!

Let's all gear up, drop all fear,
Come on, my dear!
Let's all be present here,
Enjoy, celebrate, and become sincere seers.

Nature is here to inspire,
Caring for our smallest desire.

Live in the moment,

With all your innocence.
Have patience,
For the mind is ancient,
And the soul is constant.

Live in the moment...
True brilliance arises
With grace and commitment!

The DSN Program

*The DSN Program (Dynamism for Self and Nation), is a transformational course offered by The Art of Living designed to help participants overcome personal barriers, inhibitions, and fears to access inner strength and potential.

Select References

https://www.deccanherald.com/india/assam/181-dnla-militants-formally-surrender-in-assam-2746365

https://www.indiatodayne.in/assam/story/assam-181-dnla-cadres-lay-down-arms-return-to-mainstream-701922-2023-10-28

https://x.com/Gurudev/status/1109709057332404224

https://www.facebook.com/share/v/1Gojw9B8nh/

https://x.com/himantabiswa/status/1652172051829133312

1

The Death of Doubt

From drowning in fear to floating in faith.

Diphu, India, 3 June 2017

A jubilant celebration was underway in the newly built cowshed at our Diphu Ashram. Tears welled up in many eyes as we gazed at one another—no words were needed. Something deep within every heart had melted. For all seventy-six DSN (Dynamism for Self and Nation) program participants, there was a quiet yet powerful expansion of belongingness—a shared sense of connection that transcended boundaries and differences.

An absolute inner silence accompanied joyful celebrations as we neared the completion of the DSN program. A group of tribals had shed all inhibitions. Wellesley was one of them, experiencing inner freedom. He was in deep ecstasy, feeling a peace he had never known before—one that stood in complete contrast to the means through which he had once believed it could be achieved.

The events of the previous evening had sparked a memorable beginning of real peace — a true "**One World Family**," as envisioned by Gurudev. They had witnessed the unwavering commitment of Gurudev's emissary during the Diphu river rejuvenation project. As for me, with Gurudev's Grace and Samirji's (a devout disciple of Gurudev and an old hand in the Northeast, who has spent over two decades in the tribal and rural belts of India bringing fringe elements to the mainstream) timely help, I was given a new life, filling my heart with gratitude for this second chance.

I had always been a perfectionist in organizing and executing events during my corporate days at Microsoft. The DSN program, too, was meticulously planned in close consultation with Samirji.

Diphu is a small town, graced by a beautiful river that once flowed freely through its heart; clear enough for children to fish. But over time, the river turned into a burial ground for plastic, debris, and household waste. Gradually, it shrank in size and was encroached upon due to poor planning and neglect. It could still be seen from afar, but reaching it to clean had become nearly impossible.

After much effort, I finally found a way to reach the shores of this almost invisible river, right at the cemetery ghat. Seventy-six of us came together that day, united by a shared mission—to reclaim and rejuvenate the river that once gave life to our town.

Earlier, during my liaison with the authorities the principal secretary had kindly promised to provide an excavator to support our mission. However, when we arrived for our *seva,* I was politely informed that priorities had shifted—and the excavator would not be available.

"Never mind," I told myself. "*We can do it.*" An intriguing current of thoughts churned within me. As we all gathered at the ghat, our plan initially brought chaos and confusion. Yet, the Divine had other plans. The very place where people bid their final goodbyes was now becoming the cradle of transformation.

Samir ji was going with the flow, busy managing the participants. Earlier I had asked him, "Would you also be joining us in the river cleansing?" He replied, "I will do the seva with you guys," and sure enough, he already had asked someone to bring his clothes to clean the river.

We all rushed toward the riverbank. Burnt and unburnt plastic, traces of bones and skulls, a pungent stench—along with well-fed dogs and noisy crows—all seemed to be waiting to welcome us.

A few participants were missing for their own reasons, so I gathered the ones who were there and we began cleaning the ghats. There was no real plan in place. After some urging, a few women tied their dupattas over their faces as makeshift masks and reluctantly began gathering dry leaves with tiny sticks.

I intended to clear the riverbanks, but nothing was really moving. Everyone appeared busy, yet little was being done. It felt like a collective act of pretending.

"Walk the talk first," an inner voice whispered. *Charity begins at home,* I reminded myself. I called out to Khorsing, one of the shy volunteers, and together we began stepping slowly into the narrow river.

The first steps were cold and stinking.

A few more steps... the water rose to our knees.

Two steps further, and to our utter shock, both of us were suddenly submerged!

Neither of us understood what had just happened. In panic, Khorsing pushed me down in an attempt to breathe, and I instinctively pulled him down for the same. Within seconds, we were both gasping for air.

Clinging tightly to each other, we fought to stay afloat. In those moments, I came face to face with death. My entire life flashed before me, and I felt completely prepared to let go. Khorsing made one final, desperate attempt to pull himself up while I was already submerged in the water. From the riverbank, some thought we were simply swimming.

"They're drowning!" screamed Urmila Mech, our teacher from Nagaland, her voice piercing through the chaos.

In an instant, Samirji reacted. Without a second thought, he plunged into the river. In one powerful surge, his six-foot frame cut through the water, covering a great distance. His feet struck the riverbed as he pushed both of us toward the shore, while he himself sank, gulping water.

By sheer luck, my hand caught his strong arm, and he managed to seize a solid rock beneath the surface. In a split second, summoning all his strength, he pulled us both to safety.

Samirji's quick reflexes, I later learned, was no accident; he had inherited them from his father, who had served as an army brigadier.

A profound silence settled over the place; a silence of relief, awe, and gratitude. Both of us had been saved. To everyone's surprise, I soon returned to work, and the rest followed with renewed energy. The ghats began to look cleaner, and the spark of collective enthusiasm turned into a mission for social awareness about cleanliness.

A live example of taking responsibility and team spirit was now embedded in everyone's consciousness—the twin aims of the DSN program.

As we wrapped up the day's efforts and returned for the evening *satsang* (a gathering where people meditate, sing, and reflect on wisdom), news of the drowning incident had already spread; it had become the talk of the town. All of a sudden, it was as if a veil had lifted. Most of the participants in the program realized that we are here only for a short while, and that one day, we will all have to leave this body behind.

During the *satsang,* I closed my eyes and felt an overwhelming sense of gratitude toward Gurudev as his words echoed within me: ***"Total dedication brings enormous enthusiasm and challenges and leaves no room for ego."***

Something within me had shifted. I felt as if I had been given a new life, one that was ready to serve with greater humility and purpose. The DSN program had uplifted me as a person. I was in a state of '*nimit*'—just an instrument of the Divine. ***The mind, I realized, moves between clarity and confusion, again and again. But in the state where there is no doership, only surrender, there lies the most creative and progressive expression of life.***

Looking back, I had approached a few teachers to conduct the program, but none of them were able to make it. By Gurudev's grace, Samir ji, who had just returned from a year-long stay abroad, agreed to come. It truly felt like the Master's plan was unfolding perfectly.

During the satsang, a participant asked whether Gurudev loved the Northeast. In response, Samir ji sang in six or seven languages of the region, and every heart melted in devotion.

Wellesley, once a mute spectator in the program and a silent observer, found himself undergoing a profound inner transformation as he witnessed it all. Beneath his composed exterior an unwavering commitment, an unfathomable grace, and a deep sense of renewal began to take root.

From gathering the courage to communicate to suddenly being enveloped in a wave of unconditional love, Wellesley encountered peace beyond reason. In that stillness, he realized that beyond every event lies a deeper wisdom, and this realization dissolved all his lingering doubts.

A quiet clarity began to emerge within him, as though he was gently being drawn toward something greater than himself.

Next day, a meeting was arranged between Wellesley and Samir ji to translate this clarity into tangible peace for the region and bring the UPLA back into the mainstream.

The whispers surrounding my near-drowning were not whispers of death.

They were whispers of a new beginning.

A horizon soaked in Gurudev's grace was spreading across the region, silently preparing the next chapter of our lives.

Gurudev's blessings saved my life.

2

Mental Sandwich: The Mellowing of the Militants

Faith is the beginning. Confidence is the result.

It was a late winter afternoon, the sun beginning to soften its glow. After completing my *Sanyam meditation,* I was scrolling through my phone to stay updated. A local news channel repeatedly flashed stories about some insurgent operations in Assam. The text was in a regional language I couldn't understand, so I set the phone aside and drifted to sleep.

The next morning began with our group *sadhana.* Afterwards, I picked up the book *Celebrating Silence* and opened a knowledge sheet.

"You seek until you come to the Master. Once you come to the Master, seeking stops, and blossoming begins."

That was the *knowledge point* of the day, something to reflect on deeply, to let it sink within.

As usual, I was busy with our Diphu ashram logistics, coordinating programs and attending calls. Suddenly, two people walked in and greeted me with a cheerful "Juthai." I immediately responded in the same way, "Juthai," the traditional greeting of the Dima Hasao district in Assam.

I had earlier conducted a few programs in Dima Hasao, which lies along the border of Karbi Anglong district. Many visitors often come to the Diphu ashram, so I assumed they were here to inquire about upcoming programs. I welcomed them warmly and began the conversation.

In a clear, firm tone, one of them, Mukteshwar ji, said, "We want to meet Gurudev ji. We have something important to convey to him." Their words were direct, their intent unmistakable. Before I could even respond, they handed me a memorandum and asked if they could meet Gurudev ji urgently.

As I glanced at the letterhead, I noticed a logo with two crossed swords; it was from the *Office of the Dima Hasao National Liberation Army*. I realised they were representatives of an insurgent organization from Assam.

Mukteshwar ji spoke in broken English and mentioned that the DNLA president, Etika Diphusa, wished to speak with me over the phone. He added that they had been tracking me for the past three weeks. We exchanged contact numbers, and soon after, I received a call.

Etika was humble and respectful on the line. Though he was still underground, he spoke with sincerity. I assured him of whatever support we could offer within our means.

I asked Mukteshwar ji, "Why do you want to meet Gurudev?"

He paused for a moment and replied softly, "We can tell that to Gurudev ji only."

He then began sharing stories, the history of Maata Hidimba (Maata Hidimba is a revered goddess, known as the wife of Bhima from the *Mahabharata*), Ghatotkacha (He is the son of the Pandava Bhima and Maata Hidimba), and the ancient Kachari Kingdom, weaving them into the origins of the DNLA. As our conversation deepened, he showed me one of my videos—'*From guns and grenades to garlands and gamchas*'— which had been filmed at the UPLA (United

People's Liberation Army) boot camp. 'Gamchas' are traditional Assamese scarves which are often presented as a mark of honor and respect.

In that moment, I understood clearly: they were seeking Gurudev's presence not merely to address their political or social concerns, but to fulfill a deeper longing, a spiritual awakening that could transform their path.

Mukteshwar Kemprai alias Jabba Khorong Dimasa ji was the advisor of DNLA and had a close watch on all major developments in the region. They had witnessed Gurudev's pivotal role in transforming conflict-zones; from guiding the UPLA towards peace, to facilitating dialogue between the FARC rebels and the Colombian government to end a 53-year-old conflict, and even working with LTTE militants in Sri Lanka to help them reintegrate into society.

They knew Gurudev as a global ambassador of peace, and they had come seeking his guidance. While they respected the government, there was still a deep lack of trust. I could see what was behind their demand. I could see 'faith' and a quiet hope shining in their eyes.

Gurudev says: "Faith gives you strength instantly. Faith brings you stability, centeredness, calmness and love. Faith is your blessing." And he would add, "Faith is the beginning. Confidence is the result."

I stayed composed, quietly planning the next steps in my mind.

After going through the documents and gaining a brief understanding of their demands, I called Karthik ji, Gurudev's secretary.

"Can I bring a few special friends from the Northeast to meet Gurudev?" I asked.

Without hesitation, he gave me a date. Everything seemed to be falling into place. I was moving with the flow, surrendering to whatever was to unfold.

That same evening, Longki and Wellesley from UPLA came to the Diphu ashram. They expressed their wish to personally thank Gurudev for helping them return to the mainstream. I suggested, "Why don't we go to Bengaluru and spend a few days with Gurudev?"

They immediately agreed, sealing the idea by booking their tickets on the spot. I could sense how much they were yearning for Gurudev, longing for his presence and advice, and perhaps a few days of rest and reflection at the Bengaluru ashram.

During our conversation, Longki also invited me to his wedding celebration.

"You're getting married?" I asked with surprise.

He smiled and said, "Yes, with Gurudev's blessings, I'm getting married."

It felt like a moment of quiet joy. From leading a life of struggle in the jungles to preparing for a public wedding, this was transformation in its truest sense!

As days passed, I began researching more about the DNLA. According to government records, they were the last active insurgent group in Assam; fierce, organized, and strategically positioned in the hilly terrains of Dima Hasao and Dhansiri, along the Nagaland border.

Their choice of insurgency stemmed from familiar roots: lack of infrastructure, limited access to education, and the persistent encroachment on their tribal rights. Their cadres were trained across Manipur, Nagaland, Myanmar, and different parts of Assam.

What made them particularly distinct was the presence of female cadres within their ranks, a rare phenomenon among such groups. I watched several videos online depicting their operations; they were well-versed in guerrilla warfare and commanded significant influence in the region. The visuals were intense—cadres clad in rugged camouflage, heavily armed, moving with precision and discipline.

As I delved deeper into my research on DNLA, everything began to connect with the memorandum they had handed me. The document clearly outlined their vision and objectives, mapping out the group's strategic focus.

In it, they claimed their commitment to and fight for the liberation of a sovereign, independent Dimasa Nation. The memorandum also reflected the harsh realities of their path; they had recently lost six of their cadres in a police encounter, a reminder of the risks and sacrifices involved in their struggle.

This alignment between my research and their written statement made it clear: their request to meet Gurudev was not just procedural: it stemmed from deep aspirations, a combination of grief, hope, and a desire for guidance. For peace, for closure.

In the meantime, Etika Diphusa alias Kharmindao Dimasa ji, the president of DNLA, called me. He said, "Vishnu ji, our tickets are booked, and we will meet you at Guwahati airport."

I greeted him warmly with a "Juthai" and expressed my hope to meet him in person very soon.

Over the next few days, a few unfamiliar faces began visiting our ashram. Since our ashram is open to everyone, we didn't think much of it. I had no idea that we were actually being tracked.

The growing association of DNLA with the Diphu ashram had raised suspicion within the Intelligence Bureau (India's premier internal intelligence agency, operating under the Ministry of Home Affairs to manage domestic security, counter-terrorism, and counter-intelligence). They were silently observing every movement. I remained unaware of their watch but could sense a subtle tension in the air; something was shifting, and I became increasingly sensitive to these developments.

I reached Guwahati airport, unintentionally bringing together two mutually exclusive groups from two ethnic tribes: UPLA from Karbi tribe, who had already surrendered and embraced the mainstream with Gurudev's guidance and blessings; and DNLA, from Dima Hasao tribe, who were coming to seek solace in Gurudev without any prior exposure. Neither group knew that we would be travelling together from Guwahati. I didn't think much about any resistance or tension in bringing them together. Karthikji had arranged all logistics for their stay at the Bengaluru ashram.

Much later, during my research on UPLA and DNLA, I learned that there had been a severe ethnic clash between the Karbi and Dima Hasao tribes in 2005. (An ethnic group is defined as a community of people generally recognised by themselves and/or others as a distinct group, based on social or cultural characteristics.) In this conflict, both communities became victims of political manoeuvring.

The clashes between the Karbi and Dimasa were violent outbursts rooted in long-standing movements for greater autonomy by both tribes. The immediate trigger was a series of killings, including the murder of three Dimasa drivers, which led to a retaliatory attack on 34 Karbi individuals in Charchim. This turmoil caused significant loss of life, widespread property destruction, and mass displacement.

As per our schedule, we all gathered at the Guwahati airport. Longki and Wellesley, travelling from Karbi Anglong, greeted me with warm hugs. Over time, we had become more than friends, a family of sorts. They loved and trusted me, treating me as their own brother.

As soon as Mukteshwar ji stood beside me, I noticed Longki and Wellesley exchange uneasy glances. They quickly pulled me aside and said firmly, "We don't want to meet Gurudev along with the members of DNLA." The tone was firm and unwavering.

Moments later, Mukteshwar ji gestured for me to step aside. He quietly said, "Our team doesn't want to meet Gurudev along with the members of UPLA."

I asked where his team was, and he pointed toward another corner of the airport. When I went over to greet them, I saw Etika ji and said, "Juthai!" He introduced me to their Commander-in-Chief Sudri Sorongphang alias Naiding Dimasa. Etika and Naiding had been observing us from a distance for quite some time.

They, too, made it clear; they did not wish to meet Gurudev alongside the other group. The atmosphere grew tense on both sides, and I suddenly found myself caught right in the middle, like a bridge between two worlds that were still learning to trust each other.

I firmly said, "Let's just reach first." The boarding was announced, and we queued up for our seats. I sat with the UPLA team, and Wellesley politely reminded me, "We don't want to meet Gurudev alongside DNLA members."

After some time, I moved to sit with the DNLA team. Mukteshwar ji quietly told me, "We don't want to meet Gurudev with UPLA members!"

I felt trapped in a recurring mental sandwich. A loop of clear, conflicting demands from both sides. Exhausted, I closed my eyes and began doing *Sahaj meditation*. Gradually, calmness returned, and before I knew it, we had landed in Bengaluru.

As planned, Shrikant Baronia, our dynamic AOL teacher, came to the airport to receive us so we could split into two groups. Shrikant, based in Bengaluru, was my trusted confidant and had a remarkable ability to make anyone feel at home.

It was the first time the DNLA group, straight from the jungles, had come to Bengaluru. At 9:30 p.m., the city was alive with lights and activity. Everyone was hungry, and Shrikant had already arranged for us to have an authentic South Indian dinner at Anand Adyar Bhavan, a popular restaurant near the airport.

The restaurant was crowded, but with Shrikant's politeness and quick thinking, he managed to secure a table for all of us. Since there was no other option, we all sat together, with UPLA and DNLA side by side for the first time. One could feel an uneasiness in the air.

Thankfully, as the food arrived, everyone began enjoying the meal, though the DNLA team missed having rice. Shrikant quickly ordered it, and soon their plates were filled, bringing visible contentment and ease to their hungry stomachs.

We all reached the ashram by 11:15 p.m., and our ID cards were already prepared. The UPLA team was in autopilot mode, having visited the ashram multiple times before. Shrikant personally escorted the DNLA team to their rooms, and I let out a sigh of relief, knowing everyone was settled for the night.

Suddenly, around 11:30 p.m., near the reception, Gurudev's car arrived at the ashram and stopped. He had just returned from an international tour. The moment he entered, he began conversing in Tamil with one of our ashramites.

I leaned forward and said, "Gurudev, a few special friends from the Northeast have come to meet Gurudev." I felt my message didn't quite get through, and before I could try again, his car had already left.

Nevertheless, having his darshan was enough: all my tiredness and fatigue vanished instantly.

The next morning, we all gathered together in the kitchen. Many of the ashramites we hadn't seen in a long time came to greet me. In conversation, people would ask about them, and I would reply, "They are my friends from the Northeast." They received abundance of love and warmth from everyone around.

I had hoped to show the DNLA team around the ashram, but they were hardly interested; their only focus was to meet Gurudev.

We waited together in the old Secretariat, as the meeting was scheduled to be held at the School of Yoga near the Shiva temple. Once again, the same restlessness began to surface in both groups, each wanting a separate audience. I felt completely caught in the middle, with no easy solution.

Karthik ji quickly approached both groups, exchanged greetings, and ensured everyone was ready to meet Gurudev, adorned with Karbi and Dimasa *gamchas*.

Around 5 p.m., Gurudev arrived, and we were directed to the central room. I first took the UPLA team inside. They expressed their gratitude and shared some concerns with Gurudev. With his characteristic calm and wisdom, Gurudev advised them to be patient and offered practical solutions. They received the answers they had been seeking, and with the Master's blessings, their joy knew no bounds. Gurudev, knowing them personally, asked me to continue taking care of them.

Once they finished, I began, "Gurudev…" Before I could complete my sentence, He said, "Yeah, bring your other friends." His recall of my updates from the previous night was astonishingly precise.

I went back and called the DNLA team.

Etikaji walked slowly towards Gurudev, his movements stiff, a reminder of the bullet wound he had sustained in his leg during one of the encounters. Gurudev glanced at them as they approached. Before we could speak, Etika knelt and held Gurudev's feet, looking into His eyes. "Gurudev, hum aapki sharan mein aaye hain. Humara uddhar kijiye," he said (*"We have come to you. Please guide and redeem us."*)

Etika clasping Gurudev's feet in his first interaction with Gurudev.

Gurudev quietly collected their memorandum, draped a shawl around them, and offered *prasad*. That was all. He did not utter a single word.

One of his assistants then directed me to take them back. I felt utterly confused; the profound simplicity and quickness of the encounter left me searching for understanding, while Gurudev moved on to attend other meetings. I was anticipating something else, something 'more'.

When we stepped out of the meeting hall, the UPLA team was waiting. They thanked me, their faces glowing with joy from meeting Gurudev, and then went to have some rest.

UPLA team after meeting Gurudev.

I was left with the DNLA team. What should they do now? I felt that something was still incomplete.

Suddenly, I sensed that Gurudev would be heading to the Shiva temple, which was crowded with thousands of devotees. I held the DNLA team's hands and guided them through the queue for darshan.

As Gurudev walked by, for some reason,I called out, "*Gurudev, inko course kara de kya*? Should we teach the course to them?"

Without hesitation, Gurudev said, "Haan, haan," and moved on. I let out a long sigh of relief, and a sense of completion and grace settled over me.

We had not booked their return tickets, so Karthik ji quickly arranged a 'Happiness Program' along with a 'Sahaj Samadhi' meditation session for them. Over the next three days, the DNLA members immersed themselves in the programs. The UPLA team, on the other hand, joyfully attended satsangs and followed Gurudev around, soaking in every moment.

Each morning, the DNLA group began with *pranayama* and Sudarshan Kriya. In the evenings, Sahaj Samadhi brought them peace and inner solace. It was a turning point; they were entering a completely different world.

I would take them to the kitchen, and they thoroughly enjoyed the meals. When people asked about them, I would simply say, "My special friends from the Northeast." Gradually, Etika ji and Mukteshwar ji also began greeting people warmly with "Jai Gurudev"; the stiffness had dissolved.

As the program drew to a close, I updated Karthik ji and requested another appointment with Gurudev. Though Gurudev's schedule was extremely tight, we were fortunate and were scheduled to meet Him once again the next morning.

As we waited to meet him, I quietly chanted the *Guru Pooja* in my mind. Reciting the *Guru Pooja* before meeting Gurudev is an esoteric experience. It deepens the longing and makes one feel like the Divine's most beloved. I had learned this practice from Bhanumaa.

When we approached Gurudev, Etika, with all his innocence, once again held Gurudev's feet and said, "*Gurudev, hum aapki sharan mein aaye hain.*"

Gurudev looked at him with a gentle smile and said, "*Tum to humare apne ho…* you are my own."

Gurudev inquired about their experience of the program, offered them *prasad,* and said to me, "Vishnu, take care of them. Are their tickets booked? If not, get it done through the Secretariat." I replied, "Gurudev, it's already taken care of," and we departed. A profound sense of completion washed over me; my mission felt accomplished. I knew magic had been woven.

Meeting Gurudev in person is a heavenly experience; joy wells up, and sorrow diminishes.

As we exited Ganga Kutir, I noticed the UPLA team waiting outside, standing in a queue just to catch a glimpse of Gurudev. They were still "Guru chasing," completely immersed in devotion and awe.

For the first time, Etika approached Longki and said in Assamese, "*Bhal experience aase*" (*"It was a great experience"*). They began sharing and discussing their experiences in the ashram.

Longki turned to Etika and said, "Gurudev is a messenger of God in our lives. You need to follow His instructions and blossom to your fullest potential."

He continued, "We, too, faced struggles, but with Gurudev's grace, our lives have transformed. Coming to the ashram feels like returning home again and again." Speaking in their local dialect, their conversation became a heart-to-heart exchange. I could sense their gratitude deep in my soul! The barriers had broken, and they were connected through a common thread of grace. 'Tension' had transformed to 'belongingness'.

They were inspiring and uplifting each other, and then, to my surprise, they embraced in a hug. It was a moment beyond logic, beyond words. A pure expression of connection, transformation, and grace.

The progression from avoiding each other to standing together, speaking to each other, and finally hugging, was a real-time transformation. They exchanged contact details, and

I watched in awe at the depth of change that had taken place. I saw them off at the airport, each heading to different destinations.

Even there, at the threshold of departure, they shared a second hug...a connection that had grown far beyond the periphery of the ashram.

The historical conflict between UPLA and DNLA was the main reason their old wounds resurfaced when they first met each other at the Guwahati airport. It explained why they were hesitant to meet Gurudev together initially. It was perhaps a way to preserve their distinct identities and protect the fragile sense of self rooted in their communities.

After meeting Gurudev, all boundaries disappeared; the Master had worked his magic in their hearts. Worldly love can be like an ocean, vast but with a bottom. Divine love, however, is like the sky; limitless, infinite. From the depths of the ocean, they was now soaring into that boundless sky.

My mental "sandwich" of tension had transformed into a graceful wonder. We often see only the fall of the water, but we do not witness how the ocean becomes a cloud; that is a secret. The cloud returning to the ocean, however, is visible. Something magical was unfolding, and I could only stand in awe. The grace of Gurudev had elevated our consciousness, touching hearts in ways beyond understanding.

I stayed back for two more days, walking with my Maaji near Guru Paduka Vanam. Suddenly, Gurudev's car came to a halt. An infinite rush of energy filled the moment as Gurudev called out, "Vishnu."

"Yes, Gurudev!" I responded immediately.

He handed me a box of chocolates and said, "Give this to your friends." I became the perfect postman, receiving the gift with immense gratitude.

As I recollected the past few days, my mind resonated with Gurudev's earlier instruction: *"Vishnu, take care of them."* Now, the chocolates seemed like a tangible expression of that guidance, a simple way to spread sweetness in their lives. Clarity filled me, and with a heart full of purpose, I prepared to fly back to the Northeast.

The journey of both UPLA and DNLA was a testament to the transformative power of grace. From initial distrust, old wounds, and hesitation, they moved toward trust, openness, and heart-to-heart connection. Boundaries dissolved, and what once seemed impossible became a lived reality.

Through Gurudev's presence, wisdom, and silent guidance, both groups experienced not just peace but blossoming. The DNLA, once entrenched in struggle and violence, began their path of inner transformation, while the UPLA continued to strengthen in devotion and alignment with Gurudev's teachings.

As I reflected on these days, I realized that the work was not merely about programs or logistics. It was about holding space for faith, witnessing transformation, and being a conduit for grace. From chocolates delivered as symbols of sweetness to the simplicity of a silent darshan, every moment held lessons of love, patience, and divine guidance.

In the end, it was clear: seeking ends at the feet of the Master, and true blossoming begins.

3

The Pitch Presentation

The Divine Call to Diphu: When Grace Leads, the Heart Follows.

I had just completed my YES!+ program at Patiala, India when my teacher Ramnik Bansal ji invited me to Rishikesh for an advanced course in the presence of Gurudev. Taking a break in the middle of my engineering semester wasn't easy, yet there was a quiet pull from within—a soft but unmistakable call. And thus began a journey towards the Self. It was my first visit to the Ganges in recent times.

Every evening, Gurudev would arrive for *satsang,* filling the air with wisdom and stillness. The bhajans reverberated through every cell of my being, and the *Hollow and Empty* sessions felt like time itself had paused.

During one such session, my advanced program teacher Dinesh Ghodke ji told us to meditate in nature. I wandered off and found a rock by the Ganga where the water gently flowed around it. Sitting there, gazing at the river, my mind simply stopped; I closed my eyes, and when I opened them, perhaps an hour later, I saw the golden red hue of the setting sun and no one else was around. A deep silence lingered. It felt like nature itself had meditated with me. I started walking back toward the *satsang* venue, carrying with me a stillness that words could not describe.

It was Gali No. 13, and I saw Gurudev walking toward His *kutir (abode)* from the opposite side. I was alone at the gate, and this was my first personal encounter with him. My heart raced as he approached, I instinctively touched his feet. Our eyes met for the first time—there was a depth, a recognition and a longing in my gaze that had no words.

Gurudev softly said, *"Tum aa gaye"* (You have come). I replied, "Yes, Gurudev."

He smiled and continued toward his *kutir*. That fleeting encounter filled me with intense gratitude. It was elevating, a moment where I could connect with the Guru principle. In that instant, the questions *"Why am I here?"* and *"What is the purpose of my life?"* began to unfold within me.

During *satsang*, Gurudev had said, *"No one comes to me without a reason; there is always a bigger purpose behind it."* That moment led to a realization, tinged with innocent eagerness; my purpose was beginning to reveal itself—a journey I was ready to embrace.

I completed my engineering, joined Microsoft at Hyderabad, India, and eventually also became an Art of Living teacher. Over a span of eight years, I worked under 17 different managers across the world. I was a happy-go-lucky person, and colleagues enjoyed working with me, I say with humility. Teaching the Art of Living programs gave me immense joy, as I continued my corporate responsibilities.

Every afternoon, I would call Maaji who is also an ardent devotee of Gurudev and ask, "How long should I continue working?" She would always encourage me to listen to my heart and seek guidance from Gurudev.

And each time I received my salary, my mind used to wonder, *"What should I do with this money? How can I be more useful to Gurudev?"* In those moments, memories of my first encounter with Gurudev would return, softly reminding me: *"Tum aa gaye."* That phrase became a gentle, guiding echo, shaping my choices and nudging me toward a life of service and deeper purpose.

Myself with my colleagues at Microsoft, Seattle.

My life revolved entirely around Gurudev. All my holidays, hobbies and personal pursuits were centered on him and on service projects. Over the years, we executed numerous initiatives: Project Soberman, Vote for Better India, Volunteer for Better India, Date with the Divine, Clean India Green India. And yet, there was a growing aspiration to make an even deeper, more profound difference in society. I also had the opportunity to travel with our senior teachers, learning from their experiences and dedication.

Over time, my prayer to upgrade myself for a bigger purpose intensified. There was a compelling inner call to work toward Gurudev's vision of a stress-free and violence-free society.

The presence of the Master has a transformative effect: all worries and questions seem to dissolve. I have witnessed this in my own life and heard it echoed by many of my friends; the grace of Gurudev naturally guides, calms and uplifts those who sincerely seek.

After the World Cultural Festival in 2016, on 23 March, I sought an appointment with Gurudev. The meeting was confirmed, and an excitement naturally arose. My life felt full of possibilities, and all that was needed was his blessing. Deep within, I carried a burning desire to make a meaningful difference in society.

While preparing for the meeting, I decided to create a pitch presentation, anticipating all possible questions Gurudev might ask. My experience had shown me how the mind tends to go blank in his presence, so this felt like a small way to be ready for this once-in-a-lifetime opportunity.

At Ganga Kutir in the Bengaluru Ashram, my heart raced as we arrived well in advance to meet Gurudev. When my turn finally came, I rested my head on Gurudev's lap, overwhelmed by the presence of the Master, and gently placed my single-slide printed presentation in front of him, ready to share my vision and aspirations.

My slide said:

> "No plans for marriage,
> Green signals from parents,
> 100+ programs conducted,
> Eight years of experience at Microsoft,
> Love for cows..."

Every question I thought Gurudev might ask was already documented in my little presentation. I had tried to anticipate everything... my experiences, achievements, aspirations... hoping that nothing would slip my mind when I finally sat in His presence.

My proposal to Gurudev.

Gurudev gave a quick glance at my presentation and asked, "What do you want?"

I replied, "Gurudev, I have come here inspired by you. I now want to work for Gurudev."

Gurudev closed His eyes for a moment, adjusting his nostrils with his fingers, and then gently patted my back, saying:

"Go to the North East. People are waiting for you. Speak to Divya."

In that instant, a wave of clarity and purpose washed over me. The direction I had been silently seeking was given, simple yet profound, by the grace of the Master.

From that day on, a beautiful transition took over my life, and I have never looked back. It was also a wonderful birthday gift for Maaji. As a child, I always wanted to become a postman, watching our postman deliver letters to my father, and he would sometimes pay me a tip to fetch them. It seemed like such an easy and joyful job.

Years later, Gurudev made me his postman…delivering happiness directly to people's hearts. The joy on people's faces after experiencing Sudarshan Kriya was indescribable. Gurudev blessed me to be his instrument, witnessing lives transform, and I felt honored to serve as his postman, carrying the message of peace, joy and inner freedom.

I quickly took a selfie with Gurudev, and it became my personal source of strength. Whenever I missed him or faced challenges, just looking at that photo and closing my eyes was enough to feel his presence; all worries would vanish instantly. It became my stress buster. Maaji was overjoyed, witnessing the blessings of Gurudev.

A quick selfie with Gurudev.

The words of Gurudev carry both power and grace. Soon after, I sent the world's smallest resignation letter to my corporate manager:

> *Dear Kaushik,*
> *Please accept my resignation.*
> *Keep Breathing!!*

Eventually I donated all my belongings and prepared to step into an unknown territory...without connections, without certainty. My only anchor was the blessings of my Master.

And so began my lifelong sabbatical journey to the Northeast, a leap of faith into service, surrender, and discovery.

I had never been to the Northeast before and had no clue what to expect. The initial days were manageable, but gradually the challenges intensified. The biggest hurdles were food and accommodation. I had to start everything from scratch.

There were instances where I was constantly conducting programs, moving to new places, traveling through the night, and exploring different parts of the region. By his grace, the programs kept me fully occupied.

Being new to the region, there were preconceived notions about me among some locals. Trying my best to get adapted to the local environment—getting vegetarian, non-spicy food often felt like a huge *tapasya (penance)*. Many times, I skipped meals; on quite a few nights, I had no proper place to stay. I managed to stay in dorms under unhygienic conditions, and there were days I ordered food but did not eat it, because non-vegetarian items were prepared in the same kitchen.

I slept wherever I could, on roads, in buses, in trains; yet the excitement to explore and Gurudev's words kept me enthusiastic. Survival was the only option, and each challenge became a lesson in perseverance, adaptability and faith.

Looking back, my days at Microsoft were filled with comfort and security. Now, I found myself in a completely different part of the world, where even survival was a challenge. While working on Art of Living programs, my productivity remained high, but the initial days were slow, with very little work and minimal activities. Internet connections were erratic, and I faced numerous setbacks: losses, misunderstandings, occasional insults, people feeling insecure, and plans failing again and again.

What kept me going was the selfie with Gurudev, His words echoed: *"People are waiting for you."* Someone once told me that simply doing *sadhana* was the best *seva* in the Northeast. But I wanted to go beyond concepts...to break barriers and align fully with the Master's vision, serving with both dedication and creativity.

Here, no one knew me, nor did anyone seem interested in what I was doing. Yet there was deep intention within that one day people from all over the world would come to experience the serene beauty of the Northeast.

After six and a half months of enduring rains, cold, and countless challenges, there was finally an opportunity: a Teachers' Refresher Meet with Gurudev at Sri Sri University, Cuttack.

Just before our meeting with Gurudev, I was publicly humiliated by a group of people from the Northeast, and my face had flushed red, feeling crushed and ridiculed. It was one of those moments when you burn in the fire of *alochana*—criticism— a real *tapasya (Inner austerity)* by itself. I did not do anything wrong, yet I was criticized harshly. For a brief moment, the thought of giving up arose...to hang my boots and take a long break.

My face was still red, and my mind kept circling, trying to make sense of what had happened. Exhaustion weighed heavily on me, my head aching, yet my heart longed for his *darshan*. Nearly an hour later, Gurudev looked at me and asked, "Are you happy?"

I whispered, "Of course," as a tear quietly rolled down my cheek. His eyes met mine...vast, compassionate, and infinite;

then he drew me into a warm embrace. It felt like being healed by a thousand mothers at once. A blessing deeper than anything I had ever known washed over me. His gaze soothed my weary heart like a balm, and his smile became an armor that made me feel invincible. In that embrace, his presence moved inward ... inseparable, expansive and all-encompassing.

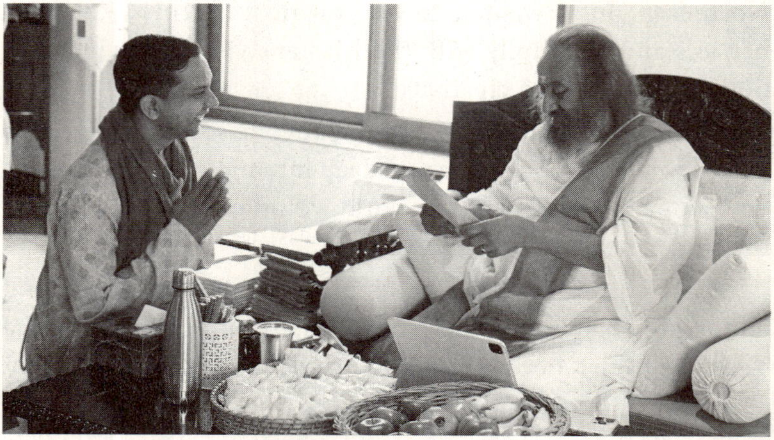

A one-on-one with Gurudev.

After a while, Gurudev left for other engagements. Bhanumaa (Gurudev's sister) later looked at me with amazement. I asked for a picture with her, and she posed happily, adding another precious memory to this transformative day.

That evening, after *satsang*, Longbir Ingti ji, an Art of Living faculty member from Diphu, Karbi Anglong, Assam, asked me, "Would you like to come to Diphu for a youth course?"

I was overjoyed; this was exactly what I had been wishing for. I had no idea where Diphu was or why I was going there, but something inside me said *yes*.

Ironically, the very people who had criticized me earlier were now amused to hear that I was headed to Diphu.

Longbirji and myself shared an instant chemistry and a common vision of the Master…it felt like Gurudev's magic was at work. After the Teachers' Refresher Meet, there was a plan in place and a meaningful engagement. This time, I was both content and excited to return, eager to share Gurudev's love and wisdom.

Something new was unfolding; another chapter in my journey, giving me yet another reason not to *hanging up my boots* and step forward. It was a Divine call to Diphu.

4

Annapurna as the Bestower

From that moment on, life forgot how to say "not enough."

Running from one place to another and keeping myself busy and productive was my mantra during my initial days in the Northeast. One fine day, Mausami Sharma, who was coordinating the rural projects of the Art of Living in the region, called me to ask if I could spend some time executing a project (about distributing solar lights in some Tengabari and Doodhiya villages where electricity was still a challenge). I was absolutely free, and without a second thought, I agreed. She cautioned me that it would be quite challenging, but I was simply grateful for the opportunity.

Mausami was working in the Upper Assam region, but she wasn't sure if we could hand over the solar battery project to the locals without ensuring accountability and responsibility. The main goal was to train the youth and empower them to take responsibility for their communities.

I booked my tickets from Guwahati to Tinsukia. After a long night's journey, I reached her place exhausted, but she welcomed me warmly with a light breakfast. Though I was tired, I agreed to begin the work immediately after eating. Having a homely meal felt like a true blessing; I cherished every bite as *prasad*.

Two young boys were waiting at Mausami's house when I arrived. She introduced me to them and handed me over to their care. We took a shared auto rickshaw to the Dinjan military station, then changed to another auto and continued our journey until we reached the banks of the Brahmaputra. From there, we crossed the river on a small boat and finally rode bicycles to a volunteer's house, where I was greeted with a warm welcome.

By then, it was almost sunset. The volunteers had prepared a meal for me, and I was so hungry that I gladly ate whatever they offered.

I was in Tengabari village in Chabua. The village's demography kept changing with every monsoon, as the Brahmaputra altered its course each time. There was no concept of electricity here; we were on a floating island with absolutely no mobile signal. When I asked about the bathroom, they simply pointed towards the river! It was an all-new experience for a city-boy like me.

My initial days in Tengabari were quite fascinating. We aimed to implement a solar battery project, but unfortunately, there were no local volunteers to help with the execution. The project held real meaning and impact. It could empower the villagers, especially the children, to study at night and bring 'light' into their lives in more ways than one.

I was clear about my goal. We wanted to train a few local leaders through the YLTP program and inspire them to sustain the solar battery project. Our Sri Sri Rural Development Programme trust (SSRDP team) had already installed a battery plant, but it wasn't operational due to lack of accountability among the locals.

According to the project plan, each household would receive two battery boxes: one for using, while the other was being charged at the station. The idea was for families to swap their batteries every day. We needed reliable volunteers who could manage the daily collection and distribution. It felt like lighting lamps for them, but my deeper mission was to ignite their inner light.

The next morning, after a light breakfast, we began going door-to-door. I met every family in the village, inviting them to join the YLTP program as we moved from one house to another. The volunteer with me translated my words into the local language. We covered every corner of the village, determined not to leave anyone out.

We received a mixed response from the villagers. Some said they were busy; others were unsure or noncommittal, using phrases like "maybe," "let's see," or "we'll think about it." No one seemed ready to commit to an eight-day program involving pranayama and meditation. Still, I continued moving from one house to another, determined to connect with everyone personally.

During the door-to-door visits, I witnessed extreme poverty. Most families lived in bamboo houses, and owning even a radio or a bicycle was considered a luxury. Their lives revolved around fishing in the Brahmaputra, their main source of livelihood and survival.

Meanwhile, we finalized a venue to start the program, a small Kaalibari (means the house, home, or abode of the Hindu Goddess Kali), where villagers occasionally gathered for social events during Navratri. After completing visits to every home in Tengabari, we moved on to neighboring villages, covering almost the entire island... sometimes on foot, sometimes on a bicycle. By evening, we finally reached the battery station and sat in silence for a short meditation, feeling grateful and grounded after the long day.

Near the battery station lived a woman named Durga Das. She came up to me and asked gently if I would like to eat something. I told her I was a pure vegetarian, and she smiled, saying, “We’ll make rice for you.”

By then, it was pitch dark, and I still wasn’t sure how many people would turn up for the program scheduled to begin two days later. I plucked a few radishes and had a simple dinner of rice and radish. That night, we returned to the volunteer’s hut, and the moment I lay down on the bed, I fell fast asleep.

The next morning, the same routine began again. By noon, I had gained confidence that the program would indeed take place. I crossed the river and went to Dinjan station, the only place where one could get a mobile signal, and called Mausami.

“We’ll have around 20–25 people for the program starting tomorrow,” I told Mausami. She sounded surprised, though not entirely convinced that so many would show up. I had always been good at planning, so I quickly estimated the grocery requirements. With the little funds in hand, we arranged provisions for eight days for about twenty-five participants, adding a little buffer just in case. Soon, the groceries reached the Kaalibari. Little did I know that I was going to witness the play of the divine, first-hand.

This was my first YLTP program, scheduled to begin at 9 a.m. After breakfast, as I was walking toward the Kaalibari, I noticed a few people heading in the same direction. We began with ten participants; within ten minutes, we were fifteen. Then, every couple of minutes, someone new arrived. By 9:30 a.m., there were about forty-two people gathered. They had no sense of exact time. Many had started their journey early in the morning just to make sure they didn’t arrive late. Most of them didn’t even know why they had come; they had simply trusted the invitation and showed up.

We began the session with “I belong to you.” The words resonated deeply with everyone. Since the villagers all knew each other, the atmosphere quickly filled with fun. Smiles turned to laughter, and soon there was a sense of togetherness.

As I looked around, I could recognize every face from my door-to-door visits. Durga, who had offered me food earlier, now played a dual role. That of an eager participant and our dedicated cook. She poured her heart into feeding everyone with love. The divine appears in many forms.

I felt truly happy and blessed. The efforts of the last seventy-two hours had blossomed into a beautiful beginning. I had a place to stay, a meaningful project to serve, and *prasad* to eat for the next ten days.

It was my first YLTP program, and I could feel a deep transformation unfolding within me! All my earlier discomforts had melted away. I was fully immersed in each moment with my participants. When we did the Sudarshan Kriya, everyone experienced something profound; tears of gratitude flowed freely. The grace of Gurudev was tangibly cutting through their lives, bringing light, peace and a sense of belonging.

Every evening, we would gather at a different hut. Each family would joyfully arrange dinner for everyone, and after the meal, we would sit around a bonfire and sing *bhajans* in *satsang*. It was a celebration of joy and devotion. It was a feeling of deep connection. The whole village seemed to be honoring Guru Tattva in their own simple, heartfelt way. With each passing day, Tengabari grew more alive, filled with the sounds of bhajans, laughter and an unmistakable current of enthusiasm.

On the third day, we even held a *satsang* on a boat on the Brahmaputra. The setting sun, the gentle waves and the collective singing created an atmosphere so divine that it felt as though the whole region was bathed in light. *Satsang* had become our shelter, a space where hearts rested and spirits soared.

As Gurudev says, *"Satsang is your shelter from the harsh and changing influences on your life. Satsang is the nest in which you can rest."*

During *satsang,* villagers would often offer me cow's milk, freshly warmed over wood and charcoal. Its taste was pure, earthy, and sacred. It felt like drinking golden elixir.

I used to wake up very early in the morning, take my bicycle, and ride to the Brahmaputra for a bath. The chilly river was invigorating, and bathing in the open was a completely new experience for me.

Durga cooked with incredible love and devotion, balancing her roles as both participant and cook. She would attend the knowledge sessions from her makeshift kitchen, letting the food simmer while meditating. It was as if she had a special gift; her cooking was not just preparing food but creating *prasad,* which she would first offer to Gurudev's picture and the Kali idol before serving lunch.

Day four went superbly; everyone was connected, no one wanted to miss even a minute. They were disciplined, longing for knowledge and *bhajans*; many transformations had already happened, their small minds had shifted to big minds. From what is in it for me, to how I can contribute to others... there was a visible change in attitude. The transformations were magnificent to behold.

When we concluded day four, I realized that every day, around 40 small kids came only for food. My estimates had been for 25 people and 8 days, and now we had almost 80 people eating for the last four days. I went to Durga and asked, do we need to order more groceries? She simply told me not to worry and just focus on the program.

Day five passed, and around 100 people were having food. Something nudged me to check with Durga again, and she calmly said the same thing: "Don't worry, you focus on the program."

A make shift camp for YLTP program.

On day six of the YLTP program, we had 42 participants, but over 120 people were eating! I panicked, imagining our stocks running out. I quickly went to Durga to assess the situation, and this time she scolded me lovingly: "*Bhaijayaji, chinta mat kijiye.*"

I simply surrendered!

After the session, I decided to check the stockroom of the makeshift kitchen myself. I was absolutely amazed. The rice sack had barely been touched, and everything else—lauki, pumpkin, cabbage, lentils, dal and mustard oil was more than sufficient. It felt surreal, as if I had stepped into a different reality where abundance flowed effortlessly.

I left with a sense of amazement, still marveling at the day's events. Nevertheless, I was too exhausted. After quickly finishing my dinner, I went to sleep.

Around 2:30 a.m., I felt a minor stomachache and urgently needed to go to the riverbank. I wrapped myself in my shawl;

it was pitch dark, but Vishal ji had given me a laser torch. I quickly freshened up at the riverbank and took a bath. Thinking of the Brahmaputra as Ganga Maiya, I took a few dips, feeling a deep sense of reverence and connection.

Returning to my bed around 3:30 a.m., I decided to meditate. Adjusting myself under the blankets, I sat quietly and began the Hari Om meditation from my phone, embracing the stillness and serenity of the night.

A few minutes into the meditation, I adjusted my blanket, stretched my body fully, and continued meditating. I was somewhere between wakefulness and sleep, perhaps in that subtle space between dream and *turiya* (meditative state).

In that state, I saw Gurudev. I walked toward him, and he extended his hand, gently leading me for a walk along the Brahmaputra. It felt as though this was something we had always done; as if every morning, we walked together by the river. I was holding his hand, walking beside him in the quiet, crisp air. The night was cold, yet perfectly still and luminous.

Gurudev looked at me and asked gently, "How are you doing?"

I replied, "Gurudev, everything is going well, but my logical mind cannot comprehend what's happening with the groceries. I had calculated for 25 people over eight days. Now, 6 days have passed, and on average, 125 people are eating every day. Logically, our supplies should have been finished by now. But when I checked the kitchen last evening, it was as though nothing had been used; the store looked almost untouched."

Gurudev listened silently, with that familiar calm smile. Then he said, "*Maine Annapurna ko keh diya hai, tumhe kabhi kami nahi rahegi.*" ("I have told Annapurna, there will never be any lack for you.")

He blessed me, and then slowly disappeared. I sat there, unsure whether I had been dreaming or witnessing a deeper reality. The meditation track had already stopped, yet my mind was still absorbed in stillness. I got up quietly and continued with my morning *sadhana*, filled with awe and gratitude.

On day seven, around 250 people were having food. It felt like a grand celebration. By then, we had trained enough volunteers who were ready to take charge of the solar battery project.

On day eight, the final day of the program, nearly 450 people came for *prasad*! The entire village was invited, and the energy was joyous and vibrant. Once the course concluded, we began winding up the program. That's when Durga came to me and asked, "What should we do with the remaining groceries?" I simply replied, "Keep them with you and continue feeding everyone."

Over time, many visitors came to the village to learn about the project, and Durga continued to serve food to all. Even to this day, many people share that she keeps up this beautiful tradition... nourishing not just the body, but the spirit of everyone around her with her delicious *prasad*.

When it was time to bid farewell, the entire village came to see me off. Tears glistened in their eyes as I prepared to leave, boarding the boat to cross from the island back to the Dinjan camp. They shouted, "Jai Gurudev! Jai Gurudev! Come again, don't leave us!" It was an emotional moment for everyone, and I, too, held back my tears.

I felt immense gratitude for the entire experience. Youth leaders were now confidently taking care of the solar battery project, and I had witnessed the true power of grace in action.

The project became a grand success and was later inaugurated by Sri Sarbananda Sonowal ji, the chief minister of

Assam! Over time, the government made further upgrades, and what had started as a small solar light initiative eventually brought electricity to the entire island.

My encounter with Gurudev that night left me with a profound sense of protection and security. Since then, I have never faced scarcity in executing any project. It felt like a direct connection with Goddess Annapurna herself... a living promise of "योगक्षेमं वहाम्यहम्." On my way back, I opened a book and came across a poem by Gurudev that perfectly echoed this experience, filling me with gratitude and reassurance.

If I had to promise you something, what would it be?
I can't promise that you would always be comfortable... Because comfort brings boredom and discomfort.
I can't promise that all your desires will be fulfilled... Because desires whether fulfilled or unfulfilled bring frustration.
I can't promise that there will always be good times... Because it is the tough times that make us appreciate joy.
I can't promise that we will be rich or famous or powerful... Because they can all be pathways to misery.
I can't promise that we will always be together... Because it is separation that makes togetherness so wonderful.
Yet if you are willing to walk with me, if you are willing to value love over everything else
I promise that this will be the most rich and fulfilling life possible.
I promise your life will be an eternal celebration,
I promise you I will cherish you more than a king cherishes his crown,
And I shall love you more than a mother loves her newborn.
If you are willing to walk into my arms,

If you are willing to live in my heart,
You will find the one you have waited forever....
You will meet yourself in my arms...
I promise.

This whole episode polished the sense of 'surrender' within me. As Gurudev says, "That which you cannot handle by yourself; that which has become a burden for you; that which you are tired of carrying on your head, just put it down and let go! That is what is meant by surrender."

Annapurna had entered my life as a Siddhi-datri (one of the forms of Goddess Durga)—a divine blessing from Gurudev, a gift received in his embrace. I felt firmly on the path of love, ready to move toward a new destination, carrying the captivating beauty and innocence of Tengabari in my heart.

Gurudev's words echoed within me: *"You cannot follow me because I am behind you, and I am in you. For long, you have been a sheep. Now it's time to be a lion."* I felt certain that something big and profound awaited me on my journey ahead.

5

The 540 Minutes

Meditating and Mediating with the Militants

I soon moved to the Diphu Ashram nestled amidst nature. The monsoon showers had elevated its charm, making it even more lush and vibrant. I began overseeing numerous civil works while also tending to our bull, Shambhu, who had been paralyzed and required meticulous care. Each task, which was a completely new experience for me, demanded patience and focus, grounding me deeply in service.

Samir ji is a naturally quiet and jovial person, yet those who know him realize that he possesses absolute clarity and unwavering commitment. I still struggle to fully comprehend his persona. Gurudev had asked Samir ji to return to Diphu, and after nearly a decade, he had relocated to the Northeast.

One evening, during an early dinner at the Diphu Ashram, with his usual fearless spirit, Samir ji gulped down an entire *bhut jolokia,* the red-hot king of chilies, in one go, enjoying it. Most people would be sneezing and gasping at even a small bite. True to his nature, he offered tiny pieces to me on my plate, grinning mischievously as I hesitated.

"Chilly brings chillness," Samir ji insisted, but I was never convinced by his theory. We were almost done with dinner, the laughter and camaraderie lingering in the air.

Suddenly he said, "I am leaving for Guwahati, and you have to be available for some important work. Reschedule your programs and wait for further instructions."

Before I could think about what to say, he had already retired for the day. His tone carried a rare blend of sensitivity and seriousness, a depth I hadn't fully encountered before. I intuitively knew something big was happening. I sat there, absorbing the weight of his words, unsure of what awaited me next.

Two days later, I received a message from an unknown number: *"Shift to Longbir's house tomorrow. Someone will receive you."*

I called back to confirm and immediately recognized Samir ji's directive voice giving instructions.

As per the plan, the next morning, I shifted to Longbir's humble abode, ready to step into the next chapter of my journey.

I have countless memories associated with Longbir's home. It was a proper traditional Assamese house, with enticing passion fruit hanging along the periphery. His garden was like a living encyclopedia, full of traditional herbs and local flowers.

Longbir's family had hosted me during my initial days in Karbi Anglong (Diphu town is in Karbi Anglong district), and they treated me as one of their own. Their warmth and hospitality made the transition to this new phase of my journey both comforting and inspiring.

A sumptuous breakfast awaited us early in the morning. Kache, Longbir's wife, was serving mouth-watering organic black rice, fresh pineapples, mango-flavored ginger, and a bowl of crisp, fresh salads. Knowing my fondness for okra, she had specially cooked the local lady's fingers just for me.

I felt completely at home. Curious about the local fruits, I asked for jackfruit... my preference had quietly shifted from mangoes to this tropical delight. It was served alongside some tangy and refreshing passion fruit juice, making the breakfast an unforgettable start to the day.

Jacong, Longbir's elder son, with his twinkling smile, told us that someone was looking for me. As I was winding up and searching for my phone, Samir ji had already called: *"No need to carry anything, not even your phone. Period."* I was surprised but decided to go with his flow.

Kache, Longbir's wife, quickly packed some food for the journey. Since I had already eaten my fill, I politely asked her to save it for later.

Before leaving, I noticed a small framed picture of Gurudev and thought of keeping it with me. Longbir sensed my intention and handed it to me even before I asked, adding a small but meaningful blessing to my journey.

The driver greeted me with a cheerful *"Kardom"*, and I acknowledged him with a respectful *"Namaste."* We started our journey along the half-paved roads of the interiors, and gradually, people passing by began hopping into our car. Within an hour, there were six of us, and suddenly, the driver was replaced by someone from behind.

We drove through the pristine natural beauty of Assam, and were fortunate enough to spot a few elephants and some elegant royal swans along the way. After another thirty minutes, I was instructed to transfer to another car, where Wellesley, Longki, and a few others were anxiously waiting, eager to welcome me and begin the adventure ahead.

"Kardom," I greeted them, looking at Wellesley, who seemed quiet and a bit uneasy. I closed my eyes as well. At first, it felt like the car had stopped multiple times, but gradually I settled into meditation.

After a journey of over three hours, immersed in stillness and observation, we finally arrived at a boot camp, ready to step into the experience that awaited us.

The boot camp resembled a proper mini-military station, guarded by cadres in uniform, many carrying weapons. From my previous experience conducting programs in army camps, the environment felt strikingly familiar. I soon realized that our slow progress had been due to security clearances from insurgency intelligence.

Everywhere, cadres were busy with their duties. Some marched with guns, others demonstrated guerrilla warfare tactics. One person was confined in a lockup, while a few others kept vigilant watch from bamboo towers, binoculars in hand. We had arrived at a training camp in an undisclosed location, deep in the jungle, possibly near the Nagaland border—an unknown world, both intimidating and intriguing.

In the past, I had always been to 'friendly' army camps; this was the first time there was an air of suspense about what might happen here. But one thing was certain and unshakable, I felt completely secure and calm from inside because I was here for 'His' work, and I just knew that I had the best possible protection on this planet.

Soon, to my surprise, a TV reporter and his assistant appeared after being thoroughly frisked at the boot camp entrance. Without missing a beat, they immediately began capturing the various guerrilla warfare tactics live on camera, adding an unexpected layer of media attention to the otherwise intense and disciplined environment.

It was clear that something significant had been planned, and I began decoding my interactions with Samir ji, trying to understand the layers behind each instruction and subtle guidance he had given me earlier:

"Vishnu, you need to stop your social accounts."

"Some projects will require you to walk on a razor's edge," he had continued.

"Avoid distractions and stay completely focused on the goal."

Mentions of nation-building, Subhas Chandra Bose, and other unsolved puzzles suddenly began to make sense to me. Piece by piece, the bigger picture was unfolding, and I felt the weight and clarity of the responsibility entrusted to me. Gurudev's words, "People are waiting for you," echoed somewhere in my heart.

"Do you need some water?" a young cadre asked, bringing me back to the moment.

"Thank you," I replied, gulping down the entire bottle. I was instructed to stay in one place, so I settled into observation, taking in everything around me.

Commands flew across the camp: *"Move!" "Quiet!" "Run!" "Position!" "Trigger!" "March!"* Meanwhile, the reporter was doing his best to capture the cadres in action. Their movements, so natural in training, now seemed almost forced and unnatural in front of the camera.

The cadres were young, innocent youths, trained to survive in the harshest jungles. They feared nothing... not rhinos, venomous snakes, pythons, scorpions, leopards, or even wild elephants. Yet, there was one thing they were truly afraid of: humans. Yes, humans!

"Humans... scared of humans?" I thought to myself. It was true, as I recollected the plight of Ramsingh, the commander-in-chief of UPLA, who had been beaten to the bone in police custody. In one of his high-profile operations, he had infamously assassinated a senior police superintendent in West Karbi Anglong a few months back.

He had been captured by the Assam Rifles at Dimapur, Nagaland, during a carefully orchestrated intelligence operation. During his prison time, I had an opportunity to conduct an Art of Living course called 'Prison-SMART', that has been designed to bring relief to prisoners. It has been conducted in various prisons in over 65 countries around the world. This program teaches skills that reduce stress, heal trauma and help them break away from the cycle of violence and negative emotions.

During an intimate conversation with me in the Prison-SMART program, he had expressed his heartfelt wish to meet Gurudev and invite His Holiness to his native place. He believed that if Gurudev came, the entire region would experience peace, guided by his divine presence.

At the boot camp, live interviews began. The cadres were visibly shy before the camera, and Longki's team was growing restless. My natural instinct nudged me to help, so I gently offered my support to Longki, and he agreed.

I gathered a few cadres and began guiding them through simple breathing techniques. "Take a long, deep breath in… hold… and breathe out." After a few rounds of *Ujjayi* breathing and three sets of *Bhastrika,* the energy around us shifted. The stiffness dissolved, their faces softened, and suddenly they were smiling… natural, relaxed and confident before the camera.

The live interviews resumed, and I found myself encouraging them to speak their hearts out. What had begun as hesitation had turned into enthusiasm.

That day, at the boot camp, something profound unfolded. As I listened, I finally understood why I was there, not by coincidence, but as a representative of the Art of Living, to bridge the hearts that had long been torn apart by conflict.

The United People's Liberation Army (UPLA) was preparing to announce a unilateral ceasefire, a historic gesture that would soon be telecast across the Northeast.

Ceasefire meant entering into dialogue with the government. After years, there would be no more violence, no more bloodshed, only a progressive path toward peace. One by one, the cadres began narrating their stories: years of armed struggle, loss, and survival in the shadows. Their words carried pain, yet a quiet hope shimmered through. They spoke of their challenges, of hunger, fear, mistrust and the heavy price they had paid. Recently, two of their comrades had lost their lives in an accident.

Samir ji was in indirect touch with Gurudev's secretariat, and he wanted me to be on the ground. Sending Gurudev's emissary into their camp was seen as a sign of trust; a welcoming gesture that deeply resonated with their top leadership. For them, it wasn't just a visit; it was a message of hope and recognition that peace was possible.

"Vishnu ji, you also come and share," insisted Longki.

Samir ji's stern warning immediately echoed in my head, *"Stay silent unless told."*

Before I could respond, Wellesley jumped in, signaling discreetly to the camera crew, trying to manage the situation. I held my breath and stayed quiet, my mind torn between obedience and intuition.

In the meantime, the cadres started murmuring among themselves in their local dialect. Gradually their tone shifted from curiosity to frustration; they wanted me to speak too. The cameraman looked helpless; the tension was rising. Within minutes, the entire recording was on the verge of being called off.

"Jai Guru Dev!" I prayed silently, closing my eyes for a moment.

In that stillness, I sensed a subtle *"go ahead"*, a green signal from Gurudev in my inner space.

The recording lights turned on. I had his picture close to my heart and his presence in my mind. Words began to flow, not from memory, but from somewhere beyond me. I started speaking effortlessly, though I had no idea what exactly I was saying. It felt as if Gurudev himself was speaking through me.

"From guns and grenades, to garlands and gamchas! Violence is not the way forward.

We have a rich history of transforming conflict into compassion. Gurudev Sri Sri Ravi Shankar ji himself has shown the world how peace can be achieved through dialogue and understanding.

We are here for you. We want to walk with you, work with you, and uplift lives together.

I invite all other groups active in the region to join hands with us; to find an *amicable and everlasting solution for peace.*

All your challenges, we will face together, with Gurudev's blessings and his message of love and unity.

May Gurudev bless you all."

"Bravo! Kurvanthu!" shouted the reporter, his voice echoing through the camp.

He had captured his best shot, my very first extempore from the heart. Suddenly, the entire atmosphere shifted. Cadres who were once stiff and silent broke into smiles and applause. Laughter, handshakes, and cheers filled the air.

For a moment, the jungle boot camp, often filled with the sounds of commands and gunfire drills, was alive with the rhythm of celebration.

Something profound had just happened. The walls of fear and separation had melted, and what remained was a sense of unity, a shared hope for peace.

Even the reporter, usually composed behind his lens, lowered his camera, eyes shining.

It felt like the Divine had scripted the entire scene.

Personally, I requested the reporter to cut my clip. He smiled and assured me softly, "Don't worry, it will be handled."

Somewhere deep inside, I trusted his words but still whispered a silent prayer to Gurudev: *"Let only what you wish reach the world."*

The cadres gathered around, their eyes bright with a strange mix of relief and curiosity. Weapons slung loosely over their shoulders now looked less like threats and more like burdens being set down.

For the first time that day, I felt the energy of the place turn gentle... as if the forest itself had exhaled.

On our way back, one of the cadres asked me softly, "Aren't you afraid of being with us?"

I looked into his gentle brown eyes and smiled.

"I trust Gurudev more than I trust myself!" I replied. This cadre had never seen Gurudev but had heard about him from his top leadership.

A pin-drop silence followed.

The air in the vehicle shifted... as if something invisible had dissolved. Fear gave way to faith.

For the next few miles, no one spoke. Only the rhythm of the road and the heartbeat of the jungle could be heard.

After nine long hours, I finally reached home. Longbir was overjoyed to see me back safe and sound. He handed me a glass of water, his eyes twinkling, and then excitedly showed me the clip: my recording with the insurgents.

By now, it had gone viral. Everyone was talking about it.

Of course, it was completely against protocol, and not all agencies were pleased— including Samir ji, who always had an eagle's eye on every development. I could almost imagine his furrowed brow and sharp gaze, analyzing every frame. Yet, despite the warnings and red tape, a ripple of positive change had already begun.

Late that night, the secretariat showed the clip to Gurudev.

He smiled a gentle, knowing smile and said, "Nice. Let the truth be shown to the world."

Over the next few weeks, the same clip kept circulating, on phones, social media, and messages from far and near. Every time I saw it, I felt a quiet joy and a deep sense of responsibility. It was no longer just my words; it had become a beacon of hope, a small step toward peace in a land that had long known conflict.

"We will not stop until the last gun is laid down across the region."

A part of Gurudev's *sankalpa* was coming alive; a quiet, determined vow taking shape in many hearts.

A few days later, Samir ji was back to Diphu ashram and said, "You nailed it, champ. Nice video."

Hearing this from him was extraordinary. Compliments from Samir ji were rare, precise, and carried immense weight. In that brief moment, I felt a quiet validation of all the uncertainty, hesitation, and effort that had gone into. It was a subtle nod that the message had landed exactly as intended.

I quickly offered him some red-hot *bhut jalukias* I had personally harvested from Longbir's farm.

Samir ji eyed them carefully, a small smirk playing on his lips, and then, with a mix of curiosity and caution, popped one into his mouth. His eyes watered instantly, and he let out a sharp hiss, but there was a spark of amusement behind it.

Wellesley was acutely aware of the turning point in their lives. Transitioning from underground to overground was no small feat…the pressure of constant intelligence agency calls, court hearings and public scrutiny was mounting.

Samir ji, on the other hand, was quietly orchestrating plans, strategizing to take this peace initiative to the next level, always thinking several steps ahead.

Meanwhile, I found my rhythm in service. Conducting programs, nursing Shambhu (our bull), who was severely ill, planning solar light distributions, enhancing the ashram facilities and preparing for the PAN-India 'Advanced Course' at our Diphu ashram.

Amid the chaos of external pressures, there was a profound sense of fulfillment. And an unmistakable sense of quiet joy in knowing that the divine has chosen me as a tool to bring peace and happiness to so many conflict-ridden lives. "Many people are waiting for you." I was beginning to understand what it meant.

6

Dhatri's GPS

What was lost to the world was never lost to love.

Staying in Assam required a lot of discipline, especially battling with the bed. Once, I travelled to Chabhua, Assam in late 2016, a small island on the Brahmaputra in Upper Assam, to conduct a YLTP Program. I stayed there for nearly ten days. With no Internet and limited electricity, it felt like I was in a completely different world.

I stayed in a *chang* house made with bamboo, where one had to go to the river to bathe or attend to basic needs since the concept of a toilet simply didn't exist. The Brahmaputra, famously the only river in India regarded as 'male', changes its course every monsoon. People there live like nomads, shifting their *kutcha (temporary)* houses each season.

One evening, while walking around, I encountered a group of beautiful local cows returning to feed their calves. Their gentle grace and affectionate presence were captivating. I paused to watch them, and in the blink of an eye, they had vanished into the evening, leaving only the memory of that serene sight.

As night fell and the cold set in, a volunteer brought me a glass of milk, heated over cow dung cakes. The taste was heavenly. Sipping it on that freezing night, my thoughts turned to the cows.

Someone shared with me, "Vishnu ji, two years ago, we had 105 cows. Now, we have only three." Shocked, I asked what had happened to the rest of them. His eyes welled up with tears as he explained that more than a hundred cows had been lost in last year's floods, but only three had survived!

Floods are a regular, harsh reality in this part of Assam. As I listened, my mind raced with possibilities. A small thought kept troubling me: what if the next flood wiped out these rare, authentic desi cows? I immediately took a *sankalpa* to take at least one to our Diphu Ashram, perched safely atop a mountain, a sanctuary for these gentle creatures.

The next morning, during a short break from the YLTP teaching session, I took a bicycle and rode toward Dinjan Military Station. After a mile and a half of cycling, I finally reached a spot where we could get a proper signal and charge our phones, ready to make the necessary arrangements.

I called Longbir ji, and to my relief, he picked up.

"Jai Gurudev! Longbir ji, I plan to bring a cow to Diphu Ashram. Do you want me to bring some cows for your farm too?" I asked. His voice lit up with excitement, and he giggled a joyful "Yes!" I simply told him, "Make a place for their stay, and I'll be back in a few days after the program."

The next day, I went to see some cows. They were beautiful, and the calves were ecstatic to reunite with their mothers after a whole day of grazing. It was fascinating — every calf can identify its mother, and every mother knows her calf. If by mistake a calf wandered toward another cow, it would get a sharp kick on the nose!

I asked the owner if I could buy a few cows. He refused flatly. When I tried to convince him it was for an ashram, he looked at me suspiciously, thinking I might be a cow poacher, and went back to milking, giving me nothing but a blank stare.

I pondered for a solution and came back the next evening, this time carrying Gurudev's photo. I said, "We need a few cows for Gurudev's ashram." Something in his tone had shifted. He finally pointed out a few cows that were sick or unhealthy. I negotiated humbly and accepted the deal.

Meanwhile, Longbir ji arranged for a truck. I had to transport the cows by boat across the Brahmaputra and then load them onto the truck. Everything seemed to be going as planned.

I had funds ready to pay the owner and asked a friend, Vishal ji, who was managing some funds that were received from some donors, to send the money immediately. The funds were sent, but due to a technical issue during India's demonetization period, the owner had not yet received the payment, even though the money had been debited from the account.

I called my elder brother, Vedprakash ji, who is a banker, seeking a solution. He patiently explained a detailed process and was kind enough to examine the transaction. Since the process was still underway, he asked me to wait two more days. I felt helpless; time was running out, and my carefully laid plans seemed to be falling apart. Yet, my intentions were pure.

With a strong prayer in my heart, I silently blessed the owner.

Suddenly, as if guided by an unseen hand, he changed his mind: "You can take the cows," he said. Surprised, I asked what had happened. He replied, "*Gurudev ke ashram me ja rahe hain, aap ache aadmi ho, paisa aa gaya hai.*"

My logical mind, filled with long technical explanations, was stunned. The money had just arrived, perfectly timed. It was divine intervention. At Art of Living, we have a popular saying, "We don't believe in miracles, we rely on them!"

More drama was in store. The cows were promptly loaded onto a boat for a two-hour journey. The moment we reached the shore and tried to unload them, they bolted crazily, as if they had planned this escape after their first boat ride. It was a scene of sheer chaos and comedy: cows versus humans in a frantic game of catch-me-if-you-can! The villagers joined in the chase, running behind the animals with shouts and laughter. In the end, we somehow managed to round them up and load them safely onto the truck.

I didn't have any official documents for transporting the cows. The driver was well-meaning, but he refused to move without proper paperwork. In the midst of the jungle, where could I possibly get a document? I looked into the driver's eyes, gave him Gurudev's picture, and said, "If anyone bothers you, show them this picture and tell them these cows belong to him." Somehow, he accepted it, placing Gurudev's picture in front of the seat, and started the journey. Gurudev's picture acted like a divine document. As I saw the truck leave, I felt an absolute sense of peace; my small intention of bringing the cows to Diphu Ashram was beginning to manifest.

After completing the program, I returned to Diphu and went straight to Longbir ji's farm. To my delight, the cows had arrived safely, without any trouble at all.

We wanted to transport one cow to our ashram. I chose a brown one, but my eyes fell on a white cow as well. She had injured her legs during the journey and needed immediate care. Longbir ji, with humility and kindness, allowed me to take both. They were inseparable, like two sisters; I knew intuitively they would thrive together at the ashram.

Our ashram team was eagerly waiting to welcome our two new family members, bringing our cow count to five. Happiness filled the air, though our cowshed now felt quite small. The cows adjusted gracefully as the rainy season slowly arrived.

For three days, it rained relentlessly... poured cats and dogs, as the saying goes ... bringing life at the ashram to a near standstill. Even the cows couldn't go out to graze. Late one night, a powerful thunderstorm struck, accompanied by torrential rainfall. We were confined to the Hemphu dorm, watching helplessly as the storm raged outside.

Four days later, the clouds finally parted, revealing a glimpse of the sun. To our surprise, the cows were grazing atop the ruins of the demolished cowshed. The thunderstorm had completely destroyed our *gaushala*. Despite the chaos, there was something profoundly awe-inspiring in seeing them calmly navigating the wreckage, a testament to resilience and nature's quiet strength.

I decided to build a proper, *pukka* cowshed and began working toward it. Priya ji, a senior Art of Living teacher, had named the brown cow Vaishnavi and the white one Dhatri. With careful attention, Dhatri's wound healed fully, and she grew healthy and strong. All our cows soon roamed freely, enjoying the open spaces beyond the ashram. But, without a proper boundary, we often found ourselves clueless about their whereabouts.

Most days, we had to search for the cows and bring them back before sunset. One evening, Kamal ji, our ashram caretaker, informed me that Dhatri and Vaishnavi were missing. I had had a very hectic day and was about to retire for the night. I assumed they would return by morning.

But the next day, they did not. Alarm bells rang. Our team searched extensively over the following days but returned empty-handed. Productivity began to suffer, with our attention constantly diverted. Our upcoming program loomed, and the *gaushala* looked abandoned — only two cows and a calf remained. The missing cows had become part of our family, and their absence weighed heavily on everyone.

Everyone in the ashram was deeply upset. Meals were being skipped, and the mood was heavy with worry. I realized we could not continue wasting entire days searching for the missing cows; we had to focus on what we could control and look forward.

Someone suggested that the cows might have been sold to Nagaland or even Bangladesh. The thought made us feel insecure and helpless. I had to make a firm decision: continue daily searches with the team, or concentrate on ashram activities. I ultimately drew a strict line. No more expeditions. I told everyone, "If the cows are meant to return, they will come on their own. Let us focus on our day-to-day responsibilities and our service."

The next morning, after *sadhana,* Kamal ji approached me with a humble request to search for one more day. Kamal ji has a way of speaking that leaves no room for refusal, he is humility personified. I could not deny him, and a small glimmer of hope returned with his insistence.

I said, "Okay, this will be the last time." Without wasting a moment, Kamal ji went to Gurudev's picture, offered a heartfelt prayer, and set out to search for the cows, guided purely by faith. He believed they were protected, only temporarily lost. With utmost devotion, he wandered randomly.

Three hours later, he called me, breathless with excitement: "Vishnu ji, I have seen Vaishnavi!"

Bingo! Awesome! Overjoyed, we all ran nearly three kilometers to bring her back. That moment brought a surge of confidence and faith to the entire team. It was living proof: prayers do work.

That same night, Kamal ji told me he wanted to go search for Dhatri. I said, "Why not?"

The next day, he once again prayed in front of Gurudev's picture and set out randomly, guided by faith. And in just three hours later, he traced Dhatri. Overjoyed, we ran another three kilometers in a different direction to bring her safely home by noon. The emotions of joy and gratitude were overwhelming. After lunch and a short power nap, I resumed my usual calls, while the team celebrated quietly and returned to their routine.

Around 4 p.m., Dhatri began howling loudly. I assumed she was still missing the freedom of the jungle, so I tied her tightly, fearing she might run away again. But her cries intensified. I felt uneasy and tied her even tighter. Over the past few days, she had lost weight and become thin, probably from insufficient food in the wild. To our astonishment, she struggled fiercely, trying to break free.

In that moment, I looked closely at her and saw milk oozing out. Realization struck me like a lightning bolt. "Oh! She must have given birth in the jungle, and it's time to feed her baby."

I felt a surge of insecurity. What if we let her loose and she ran away? How would she find her newborn in the dense jungle, that too with sunset approaching? Insecurity makes one defensive, and this defensiveness often blocks the blossoming of trust and miracles.

With a deep prayer, I tied a long rope to her and instructed the team to follow her, though I wasn't sure she would locate her baby. The moment I released her, she bolted as if for her life, running recklessly through the fading light. Our team followed, and soon it became pitch dark in the cold winter air.

After twenty-five minutes of running, she finally stopped near a bush, repeatedly returning to the same spot. We had no idea where we were. Then, near Mijung village, she made a peculiar call: *"Eain, eain, eain…"* From the bush came another reply: *"Eian, eian, eian…"* It was like an OTP exchange between mother and child!

To our amazement, a baby emerged from the bush, responding with its own "Eain, eain." Dhatri immediately recognised her calf, nuzzling it gently. Tears of joy welled up in all of us. We had witnessed a living miracle unfolding in real time, guided by instinct, love, and the unmistakable hand of the Divine.

It was a moment of pure rejoicing. With just the GPS of love, the mother had found her newborn, and the baby had recognized her mother. It reminded me of Gurudev's words: *"Love is not an emotion, it is our very existence."*

I watched in awe as the celebration erupted. I lifted the newborn in my arms and carried it lovingly back to the ashram, with Dhatri joyfully following, ensuring no one approached her baby except me. Delighted, a profound sense of wonder filled our hearts.

We returned to our *satsang*, which felt even more intense and prayerful.

And so, Sita was born. Our little family had grown to six. She taught us complete surrender and instilled discipline, especially with time management. If we were late for *sadhana,* she would start howling for her milk, reminding us of the importance of timely action. Her presence brought structure, joy, and accountability to everyone at the ashram.

A few days later, Kamal ji called me and, somewhat hesitantly, said, "Vishnu ji, Sita is actually not Sita."

I asked him what he meant. He repeated, "No… Sita is not actually Sita."

I was completely confused.

Just then, Brahmachari Atmachaitanya ji, who was visiting our ashram, took the phone and said, "Vishnu, your Sita is not Sita—it's actually a boy."

I laughed and asked, "Are you joking?"

He replied with great confidence, "If it's not a boy, I'll owe you a treat."

Still unsure, I asked Jirsong to check. Jirsong immediately confirmed that the baby was indeed a boy and not a girl.

I was deeply upset, realizing the mistake we had made in naming the baby boy.

Later, I rang Priyaji and shared my concerns. She burst out laughing and said, "Then it's even better… we'll rename Sita as Lakshman."

And just like that, we had a Lakshman.

Dhatri with Lakshman.

At Art of Living, every situation becomes an opportunity to celebrate. As Gurudev says, *"Life is love, life is joy, and life is an eternal celebration."*

And so, the celebrations continued.

The miracle of Dhatri's GPS, of miraculously finding her calf in the dark of the jungle, became a living reminder for Gratitude, Prayer and Surrender.

7

Hippo, from the Land of Hippo

The effort to arrive dissolved the moment I felt held.

It had been a good time for me in the Northeast, and I was eagerly looking forward to the Navratri celebrations at Bangalore Ashram with Gurudev. I had already planned to attend the Silence Program there and had booked my tickets well in advance. Navratri with Gurudev has always felt like a divine call… something I have been blessed to experience year after year. It is my sacred, preplanned vacation, a time to return home within.

Just before Navratri, we received the message that Gurudev would be the state guest of Assam and would address a *Chintan Shivir* in Kaziranga for government officers. To my surprise, Gurudev was scheduled to travel back to Bengaluru from Assam on the very same day I had booked my tickets long ago.

What felt like a coincidence was clearly his design. I immediately checked with Karthik ji, Gurudev's secretary, to see if I could accompany Gurudev on his return. He said he would get back to me. It was a delicate situation; the chartered plane had limited capacity and was already full. The chances of the flight having an unoccupied seat were slim.

I prayed deeply and surrendered to Gurudev's will. After all, I was returning to be with him, and that intention itself felt complete. I dropped the thought and left it in his hands.

Gurudev was flying from Gujarat to Jorhat, Assam. The government had arranged for him to be airlifted to Kaziranga by helicopter, but Gurudev, in his simplicity, chose instead to drive from Jorhat to Numaligarh and then proceed to Kaziranga.

Kaziranga lies adjacent to our Diphu Ashram. Known for its majestic one-horned rhinoceroses, Kaziranga is a UNESCO World Heritage Site and one of India's most celebrated wildlife sanctuaries. It is home to nearly two-thirds of the world's population of the Indian one-horned rhinoceros, making it a vital conservation area. The park also shelters a rich diversity of wildlife, including tigers, elephants and wild water buffaloes. It has the highest density of tigers among all protected areas. It's truly a sanctuary of nature's grandeur.

The name *Kaziranga* is said to have originated from a Karbi tribal woman named *Kajir Ronghangpi,* lovingly remembered as *"The Rhinoceros Lady."*

According to oral history, Kajir Ronghangpi was taken from the earth to the abodes of the gods and goddesses. Blessed with divine powers, she later returned to earth in search of her earthly parents and her brother, Khoi Ronghang.

It is believed that she brought paddy seeds and a rhinoceros with her, intending to plough and rejuvenate the land. Legends say that Kajir rebuilt her father's territory in and around what is today known as Kaziranga National Park. Eventually, she returned to the heavenly realms, leaving behind the rhinoceros, a sacred reminder of her divine visit and an eternal symbol of Kaziranga.

Returning back to our narrative, the news of Gurudev's surprise visit spread like wildfire among devotees across the Northeast. Longki Bey, the founder of UPLA, called me soon after to confirm it. His voice carried both joy and longing; he was eager to meet Gurudev after a long time. We decided to drive together from Diphu Ashram to receive Gurudev at the Jorhat Airport. Longki even volunteered to drive Gurudev to Numaligarh himself.

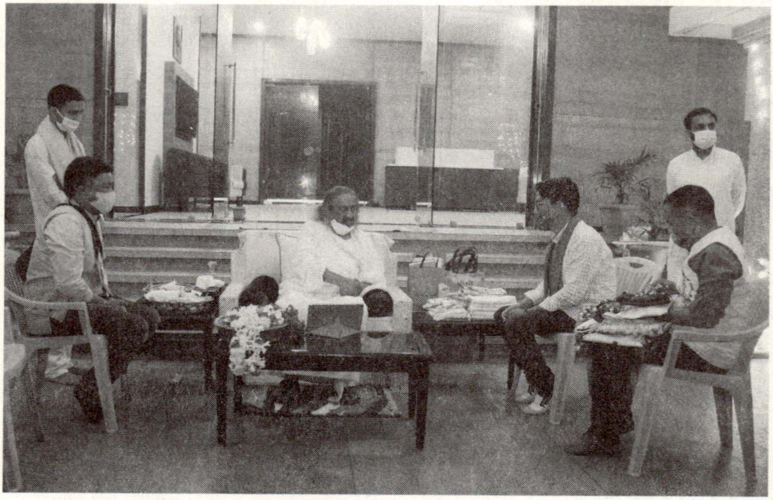

A private meeting with Longki and his team with Gurudev.

As we drove through the serene, rolling landscapes of Karbi Anglong, Longki suddenly stopped his car and pointed toward a nearby hill. "Vishnu ji," he said, "just about ten kilometers inside, we once had one of our boot camps."

"Boot camp?" I repeated.

"Yes," he replied, "that's the very place where we used to hide out in the jungles and carry out our military operations."

As we drove, Longki began to open up about his past. He shared how he was personally trained in Nagaland and Myanmar, how they would cross international borders, risking their lives, to return to India. They raised funds through extortion and self-help groups, he said quietly, and several of their cadres had lost their lives during training and operations.

As he spoke, I got goosebumps listening to the struggles they had endured. They had once taken a vow not to see their families until they accomplished their mission of peace. They were never afraid of leopards, tigers, bears or snakes, but they lived in fear of humans. Imagine that: humans afraid of other humans.

As we continued driving, a few villagers along the road greeted Longki warmly, and he responded to each of them with deep affection. He shared that these very villagers had supported them during their underground days, secretly providing food and shelter when they needed it most.

He said softly, "If Gurudev hadn't come into our lives, we might still be struggling in the jungles, fighting for the signing of the memorandum of settlement with the Indian government." His eyes glistened, and as he spoke of the Master, his voice choked with emotion.

Before we knew it, we had already reached Jorhat Airport, much earlier than expected. Though we had plenty of time, Longki had insisted that we arrive as soon as possible. In his eagerness to meet Gurudev, he even skipped his meal without a second thought.

We were brimming with excitement. I had received special permission to go inside the airport, which was a military-operated zone, but those accompanying me were denied entry at the last moment. Longki, though stopped outside, was content and filled with anticipation. Together, we prayerfully awaited Gurudev's chartered plane to land.

The moment Gurudev's plane touched down, the atmosphere transformed into a festival. Bhajans filled the air; thousands of devotees had gathered outside the airport gates, their hearts dancing in joy.

As Gurudev entered the arrival hall, I greeted him with folded hands. He looked at me with a hint of surprise and warmth. Bowing, I softly said, "Jai Gurudev," and leaned closer to whisper, "Gurudev, our special friends would love to drive you. *Gaadi ready hai… our vehicle is ready.*" Gurudev smiled gently and nodded in agreement.

But the very next moment, he was surrounded, almost "hijacked," by government officials. As they escorted him toward the protocol vehicle, he turned back, looked straight into my eyes, and said with a smile, "Vishnu, *inke saath hi jaana padega… I need to go with them.*"

It was clear, he was the state guest, and the government protocols had to be followed. Yet, that brief glance and his words were enough to fill the heart with grace.

A grand caravan of nearly 30 government SUVs accompanied Gurudev's vehicle, and soon, all of us devotees joined in what felt like a sacred chase: *Guru chasing!* There is a unique joy in following the Master's car, feeling the pull of his presence ahead. Every few meters, security personnel stood facing away from the road, ensuring that Gurudev's passage remained smooth and undisturbed. We felt immensely blessed to be part of this divine convoy.

Meanwhile, Longki was joyfully experimenting, overtaking other devotees' cars and being overtaken in return, as if it were a playful procession of love. In the midst of this, my phone rang. It was Prashant Nair ji, a senior Art of Living teacher, who was travelling with Gurudev.

"Vishnu, you are travelling back with Gurudev. Send me your ID card," he said.

For a moment, I was speechless. My heart leapt with gratitude, my prayers had been answered even before I had fully asked!

'Sarvadhi sakshi bhutam'... The Guru tattva knows every mind!

Internally, Prahshant Nair ji's message stilled every trace of restlessness in me. The urge to chase after Gurudev dissolved into quiet gratitude. I felt completely at peace, deeply thankful for the grace of this opportunity.

Gurudev often says, *"Prayer finds its way into our lives during moments of utter helplessness and profound gratefulness. A prayerful life is truly fulfilling."* In that moment, I truly understood those words.

With a heart full of joy, I turned to Longki and shared the news, "Gurudev is taking me back tomorrow!"

He was overjoyed to hear the news and continued enjoying the *Guru chasing* with childlike enthusiasm. I, meanwhile, sat back, simply breathing in and out with a deep sense of gratefulness.

A gentle stillness arose within, and the 'witness consciousness' came alive. I watched as everyone raced behind the Master's car, longing for a glimpse, including our dear Longki. Yet, within me, there was no rush, no craving, only a quiet contentment, knowing that his grace was already within me.

Gurudev stopped at Numaligarh and held a beautiful *satsang*. He was visibly moved by the love and devotion of the people, and with a radiant smile, invited a few devotees to come up on stage. One of them offered an Assamese *Jhapi,* a traditional hat and symbol of respect and honor.

People had stood in long queues for hours, yet their faces glowed with joy. The entire atmosphere was festive, filled with songs, laughter, and devotion. At Gurudev's request, the *satsang* team began singing Assamese *bhajans,* and the whole gathering swayed in bliss.

Late that night, Gurudev proceeded to Kaziranga for the *Chintan Shivir*. The event was telecast across the entire Northeast and brought an immense wave of positivity. It inspired a renewed sense of happiness, clarity and productivity among the government officials of Assam. Chief Minister Dr Himanta Biswa Sharma himself was deeply touched and delighted to have Gurudev address the Shivir.

I received further instructions from Prashant ji to reach Jorhat Airport early and complete the check-in formalities. Having travelled with Gurudev before, I was familiar with the process and felt at ease.

To my delight, I learned that our very own Rajaque ji would also be accompanying Gurudev on the return journey. Rajaque Rahman ji, a journalist turned full-time travelling teacher from Manipur, had joined at the last moment, unprepared, with just a single pair of clothes!

Since the charter was fully booked, two devotees had graciously volunteered to give up their seats. They lovingly surrendered the chance to travel with Gurudev, admitting they needed rest after the intense schedule and would rather have some much-needed sleep.

It is almost impossible to keep pace with Gurudev, who travels to nearly forty countries each year. The news of his return spread like wildfire, and devotees who had missed seeing him earlier now rushed to Jorhat Airport. Many brought food, *gamchas,* letters and small gifts for Gurudev, and entrusted them all to me. My hands were overflowing, and so was my heart. I felt immersed in the present moment like never before.

But as time passed, a wave of restlessness began to rise. Thoughts of uncertainty crept in: *What if Gurudev goes directly to Bengaluru? What if the security stops me?* My mind fluttered between faith and doubt, even as my heart held on to prayer.

Rajaque ji was quietly observing the play of my little mind. Smiling, he said gently, "Just relax." Then, in his calm and grounded way, he added, "Our love and faith must be deep-rooted. Once we realize how truly blessed we are, all complaints and insecurities dissolve, and what remains is gratitude, contentment and peace."

I smiled, feeling a wave of calm wash over me. I thought to myself, *how fortunate I am to have such a friend and guide in my life.*

And then, the moment finally arrived. We were a little late, Gurudev was already seated inside the charter plane when we boarded. As I stepped in, juggling the heavy bundles of food, *gamchas* and letters from devotees, both my hands were completely full.

Seeing me struggle with all those offerings, Gurudev looked at me and smiled, saying, "*Tu Annapurna ko le ke aagaya!* (You've brought Annapurna with you!)."

I replied with folded hands, "*Gurudev ke devotees ne diya hai (Devotees of Gurudev have offered this with love).*" Gurudev's face lit up with joy, and laughter filled the cabin.

As the plane took off, I found my seat diagonally behind him. My eyes remained fixed on him, like Nandi gazing unwaveringly at Shiva: steady, utterly content and fully in the moment.

As soon as the plane took off, Gurudev closed his eyes and slipped effortlessly into meditation. A serene stillness filled the cabin. Prashant ji handed me a paneer roll, saying softly, "Have something to eat." Though I was hungry, I humbly declined, as there was no way to wash my hands, and my heart wished to touch Gurudev's lotus feet first. I was a little nervous too, determined not to make even the smallest mistake in his presence.

But Prashant ji gently insisted, so I accepted the packet and kept it aside. A moment later, Gurudev began eating as well. Then he turned toward me with that ever-loving smile and said, "*Vishnu, kha lo bhai.*"

That simple sentence, filled with love and grace, marked the beginning of the most auspicious and divine journey of my life: travelling with the Divine.

After about an hour, Gurudev called me to sit in front of him. I was on cloud nine. Sitting there, I gazed at him in silent awe. Gurudev watched me, and I watched Gurudev, nothing else seemed to exist. In an airplane, there isn't much to do outwardly, yet inwardly, an entire universe unfolds.

Head-to-head communication happens through words and thoughts.

Heart-to-heart communication flows through feelings.

But soul-to-soul communication, that happens only in silence.

And in that sacred silence, time itself seemed to pause. After a few minutes, I began silently reciting *Guru Pooja* in my mind, eyes open, resting on Gurudev's serene form, a living embodiment of divinity in front of me.

In *Guru Pooja*, there are eighteen times when we chant *"Shree Guru Charan Kamalebhyo Namah."* And each time I reached that sacred line, Gurudev would gently blink his eyes, as if acknowledging every salutation. It was as though the prayer and its blessing were happening simultaneously, perfectly in sync. It was magical.

When the *Guru Pooja* was complete in my mind, Gurudev slowly stretched out his lotus feet, and I bowed to take his blessings. The timing was divine, flawless. That moment felt eternal, overflowing with infinite gratitude. It was as if Gurudev had gifted me his personal time for lifetimes together. The longing for his nearness melted completely; the craving had finally found its rest.

Then, with his trademark playfulness, Gurudev lightened the atmosphere. He laughed, joked, and made everyone feel utterly at home. Truly, it is said there are many forms of devotion, and in that moment, every shade of it came alive.

Saamipya, feeling the nearness, is the first step on the path of devotion. When someone is close to you, communication becomes effortless and natural. They understand your mind without words. All concerns dissolve, and a deep sense of belonging arises.

The next level is *Sannidhya,* feeling the presence. It is a meditative state where you experience that the Master is with you. Often, people realize this presence only after losing someone, but for a *sadhak,* it is a living, conscious experience. Temples are built precisely for this, to help one feel the divine presence. When you stand before the deity, you begin to sense that subtle energy surrounding you.

Then comes *Saaroopya,* assuming the form of the one you adore, where no difference remains between the devotee and the Divine. You begin to reflect the same qualities, the same fragrance of consciousness.

And finally, *Sayujya,* complete union. Here, the thin veil between the finite and the infinite dissolves. The individual merges into the Guru Principle itself…One without a second.

In that sacred silence on the plane, Gurudev's glance carried me through each of these stages. His presence drew me inward, closer and closer, until I touched that stillness where the self and the Master were one.

Time was flying, and when one is in love, time truly flies. Gurudev enquired about our service projects, the devotees, our special friends, and the Diphu Ashram. Then, with his characteristic compassion, He began sharing insights that felt like pearls of timeless wisdom.

Seeing the world through the Master's eyes, from amidst the clouds, was an experience beyond words.

Gurudev said, "Knowing that you are here for divine work fills you with strength and enthusiasm. But when you get caught up in *'me and mine,'* your energy begins to drain."

He continued, "The river may be vast, but even a small sip quenches your thirst. In the same way, accept just a little of everything in life, and it will bring you fulfillment."

His words were simple, yet profoundly deep; each syllable seemed to touch the soul, leaving an echo of peace within.

At one point, I humbly requested Gurudev to have some of the food that a devotee had lovingly sent. He took a small portion, tasted it, and then handed the rest to me. It felt like *prasad* from Annapurna[1] herself, sacred and overflowing with grace.

Gurudev then playfully posed with the *gamchas* so that I could share the picture with the devotees who had sent them. He also took all the letters I was carrying for him, each one offered with devotion.

When I conveyed this to the devotees later, many had tears of gratitude, their hearts touched by the fact that Gurudev had personally received their love.

As we began to descend towards Bengaluru, I gathered the courage to make one more humble request, to take a picture with Gurudev.

Gurudev smiled and said, "You already have so many pictures with me, don't you?"

I replied softly, "Gurudev, *charter wala* nahi hai."

---

1 Goddess of food

He laughed and said, "Yes, let's take a *charter wala* picture then."

Charter wala picture.

Prashant ji clicked the most perfect shot; it was timeless and full of grace. In that moment, the feverishness to capture more pictures with him dissolved completely.

In my realization, Gurudev does everything only to make his devotees happy. We often believe we are doing *seva* for Gurudev, but in truth, it is he who constantly does *seva* for us, out of boundless love and compassion.

In the *Ramayan,* it is said, "*Apna man tale tal jaye, par bhakt ka man na talte dekha; Prabhuji ko niyam badalte dekha.*" *(The Lord may change His own course, but never that of His devotee.)*

While deboarding, Gurudev gently enquired how we were returning to the ashram. He personally thanked the pilot and the air hostess, and even paused for a quick photograph with the crew on the ground. Gurudev treated everyone, from the highest to the humblest, with such love and dignity. That day, I learnt what true greatness looks like. It shaped me too.

The moment Gurudev stepped out, the sun was blazing bright; yet, around him, I witnessed something magical. In a radius of nearly five feet, there was a gentle shadow, while everywhere else, the sunlight was sharp and intense. As Gurudev walked towards the car, the gentle shadow moved along with him, as though nature itself wished to serve. The moment someone came forward with an umbrella, the shadow dissolved, and once again, the scorching sun filled the space.

I had heard that Gurudev has *samyama*[2] over the elements, but that day I witnessed it with my own eyes. The more we come to know him, the more we realize how little we truly know about him.

Presenting Hippo to Gurudev at WCF 2023.

---

2 Mastery, control

We all reached the ashram for the grand Navratri celebrations. But for me, Navratri had already been fulfilled; as Gurudev says, *"Jarurat se zyada aur samay se pehle sab milta hai."*

With my heart overflowing with pride and gratitude, Rajaque ji and I followed Gurudev towards the ashram. It was time for deep rest, silence and inner reflection.

A few years later, I had the joy of presenting a one-horned rhino figurine to Gurudev at the World Culture Festival 2023 in Washington D.C. Gurudev received it with a playful smile and said, "Hippo! From the land of Hippo!"

In that lighthearted moment, every memory from those divine days all came flooding back. I stood there, filled with a quiet wonder and deep gratitude. Some journeys never end; they simply blossom again in grace.

8

The Real Boot Camp

The path of love reveals itself quietly within.

Our Diphu Ashram entrance road was under construction, but the contractor's work was irregular; one day, the workers would show up, and then they would disappear for the next three or four days.

This on-and-off progress caused a lot of inconvenience, and the work just didn't seem to move forward. I had repeatedly requested him to expedite the work. Each time, he would agree enthusiastically, making big commitments, but it always turned out to be just lip service, and he would come up with polite excuses. I simply wanted to see this project completed, but at that point, I had no idea when that would actually happen.

During my meditations, Gurudev's words *"Take care of them"* would keep reverberating in my mind, again and again. But I had no idea how I was to do it.

Then, one evening, I called Mukteshwar ji and suggested that we conduct a Sudarshan Kriya for the DNLA team; I even offered to come over to their place. To my surprise, he had been thinking along the same lines and asked me for a little time. After that call, I got caught up with other programs and activities, and honestly, this thought slipped from my mind.

Nearly four weeks later, my phone rang, It was Mukteshwar ji. His voice carried a spark of excitement as he said, "The Art of Living program is ready for our team!" At that moment, everything aligned. We fixed the date, and I began preparing for it... a journey into an unknown territory,

I didn't know what awaited me there, but something within whispered that this trip is essential.

Mukteshwar ji had said he would pick me up from our Diphu Ashram, and my next few days were to be completely dedicated to them. They had worked tirelessly to bring their cadres together at the Dhansiri boot camp base. Through their own intricate network, trained militants of the Dima Hasao National Liberation Army had been called in from across the region.

As I packed the few essentials, a quiet blend of anticipation and calm settled in; this wasn't just a program, but a meeting of two worlds: one of silence and *sadhana*, the other of struggle and survival.

Many of these cadres lived deep inside the jungles, in hidden shelters. It often took a long time for any message to reach them. Some had to travel miles through steep hills, muddy paths, and thick forests just to reach the boot camp. It was truly a Herculean task to bring them together, yet their commander-in-chief had done a remarkable job. And imagine, all this was done without phones, without any network or signal.

I was filled with excitement as we set out. We began our journey toward Dhansiri, a place bordering Nagaland, Dima Hasao, and Karbi Anglong. Winter had just begun to touch the air. The ride started smoothly, winding through the jungle's pristine beauty... dense forests, elephant corridors, and nature in its untouched form.

As the sun dipped below the horizon, dusk began to wrap the landscape in silence. The roads soon turned rough, and our Bolero started swaying left and right along the ghat stretches. The stillness of the forest was broken only by the rumble of the tires and the steady rhythm of my heartbeat—part awe, part anticipation of what was ahead.

After some time, the road almost disappeared. The Bolero jolted and lurched forward, struggling to find its way through the rocky trail. Our driver, seasoned and confident on this route, handled it with ease; but for me, it felt like being on a never-ending roller coaster.

Along the way, another passenger joined us: Thausen, the commander-in-chief of the DNLA himself. His presence was quiet, steady, and carried its own authority. The road, however, had its own way of welcoming us; clouds of dust rose from every turn, covering us completely. By the time we reached the next stretch, it felt as though we'd taken a full flour bath!

As we made our way toward Dhansiri, Mukteshwar ji, the advisor of DNLA began sharing from his heart.

"It's been so many years," he said softly, looking out through the dusty window, "and yet we still don't have even basic infrastructure. Education, healthcare... nothing has really been set up for us. Look at where we stand after seventy years of Independence." His voice carried both pain and pride. "We ran from pillar to post, but everyone we approached turned a deaf ear. That's how the idea of the DNLA was born—to preserve our ethnic identity and dignity."

And then he suddenly changed the topic. "Vishnuji, we are giving you a lot of *kasta* (trouble), aren't we?" he asked.

I smiled and replied, "Not at all, I'm totally comfortable."

He looked at his colleague and said, "You are our guest," then spoke something in the local language. The two of them discussed for a while, and I sat there wondering what it was about.

After a moment, he turned back to me and said, "Since you are our guest, we have arranged *judima* and special pig meat for you."

I thought he was joking and just teasing me. But he continued, "I know you are a vegetarian, but you have to drink *judima* with us."

His tone was serious; it was more of an instruction than an invitation.

I asked, "What is *judima*?" The commander-in-chief's face brightened. "*Judima* is an indigenous wine," he said with pride. "We offer it to our guests to show respect and to celebrate."

"Mukteshwar ji, you know me," I replied gently. He smiled and, almost playfully, said, "Yes…but I am asking only for *judima*." The tone shifted: the commander-in-chief became insistent, explaining that they simply could not let a guest leave without honoring their custom. They spoke together in their tongue; I stayed silent, listening. When they repeated their request, I met their eyes and spoke plainly: "Mukteshwar ji, you may take this body, but it will not eat meat or drink. I cannot drink." The sentence hit the room like a full stop. The discussion ended.

As we made our way through the rough terrain and darkness, Etika joined us. He greeted me with sincere warmth and respect. By nightfall, we had reached our destination.

Mukteshwar ji still seemed upset, but Etika handled him gently; I sensed he was trying to calm things down and perhaps convince me about the *judima* later. They took me to a forest guesthouse where I was the only guest. A local cook was assigned to prepare food for me, but after glancing through the kitchen, I quietly decided to skip dinner.

The next morning, we were to travel by a vehicle to the boot camp, and I was all set and ready for the journey ahead.

I realized we had to start very early that morning. The air was freezing, and a thick mist wrapped the forest in silence. Someone was already waiting for me outside the guesthouse. He greeted me with a respectful *juthai (greeting)*, and together we prepared to leave for the DNLA boot camp.

We set off through the dense jungle; the path was rough, and the fog made it hard to see even a few feet ahead. After about thirty minutes of travel, we reached a bamboo sliding check post guarded by two armed personnel. They had already been informed about my arrival, and we were allowed to pass.

The camp lay deep within the forest, in a clearing where many trees had been cut. A few containers of water, some groceries, and a small chicken cage ... simple, raw and silent ... a world far from everything familiar.

After a short wait, I heard a familiar voice. "Jai Gurudev, Vishnu ji." It was Etika. Joy rose in my heart, and I hugged him warmly.

He said the boys would be arriving soon. We took a quiet early-morning walk together, sharing a quiet, intimate conversation. The cold breeze made me shiver a little, but Etika seemed perfectly at ease; he was calm and grounded, as if the chill didn't touch him at all.

The air was cold, and someone brought us a glass of hot water warmed over charcoal. As I wrapped my hands around it, Etika spoke softly.

"I'm so sorry to trouble you."

I smiled. "Not at all. I am completely comfortable."

As we stood there in the quiet morning, he shared how much he missed the days at the Bengaluru Ashram. "We'll go again," I assured him. He then asked about Gurudev ji and requested for his blessings.

As we continued our light conversation...just a simple, heartfelt talk...I found myself relaxing completely. The chill, the jungle, the distance...everything began to feel like home.

Etika then asked quietly, "Vishnu ji, do you think discipline is important?"

"Of course," I replied. "Discipline is very essential."

He nodded and said, "Sometimes we give punishments."

I responded, "Yes, punishments can also bring discipline."

Then his tone became graver. "You know, we cannot allow people to be indisciplined. I don't like those who don't follow our organization's rules," he said firmly. There was clarity and conviction in his words. After a pause, he added calmly, "I know it's not in my hands, but sometimes...we give capital punishment."

He looked straight into my eyes, completely at ease. I was stunned. How effortlessly he had moved from speaking about the *Art of Living* to the *art of killing*. I held his gaze, took another sip of hot water, and felt my throat tighten. Still, I stayed composed, steady in silence.

Inside, a storm of thoughts began to rise. I had heard about such things, but to hear it so casually from someone who once walked the same path of devotion felt unsettling. Yet, I reminded myself—judgment was not my prerogative. My presence here had a purpose, and I had to remain centered.

I slowly placed the glass down and said softly, "Etika, every life is precious. Discipline is important, yes; but compassion is greater."

He listened, his expression unchanged, perhaps weighing my words in silence. The morning fog still hung over the camp, wrapping everything in a stillness that matched the moment between us.

Somewhere within, I could feel Gurudev's grace—steady, guiding, and watchful. I knew then that whatever was to unfold in this camp, I had to remain in awareness and peace.

A little later, Etika's tone softened. He shared that he wanted to give up the idea of capital punishment and walk on the path of non-violence. It was as if a burden was lifting off his heart; he was speaking with rare openness, and I simply listened, patiently, without interrupting.

He spoke about his days in the jungles, of how people there lived in constant fear, not of leopards, elephants, or snakes, but of other humans. His voice carried the weight of memory as he described their hidden world: man-made jails dug deep into the earth, where those who broke rules were given only one meal a day. Some were fed local poisons, others were shot in the leg and left tied in the forest as punishment.

He was revealing the harsh reality of their world, a reality carved by fear and survival, yet now touched by the faint yearning for peace.

As he spoke, I felt a deep stillness within me. His words were not just stories; they were echoes of pain, of lives entangled in violence and helplessness. I could sense that behind his hardened expressions lay a longing... a longing to return to innocence.

I listened without judgment, allowing his truth to unfold. When he paused, I gently said, "Etika, every soul seeks peace; the path of non-violence is not weakness; it's the greatest strength."

He looked at me quietly, as if those words had touched something inside him. The jungle around us was silent, only the faint sound of leaves rustling in the morning wind. In that silence, I felt Gurudev's presence enveloping us—soft, invisible, yet powerful.

Someone approached, saluted Etika, and reported that the men were ready for the program.

Etika turned to me and said, "Take care of the boys." I walked into a storeroom and found about forty-eight cadres standing in military uniform, lined up and waiting. Two armed guards stood watch at the entrance.

They looked puzzled; none of them knew why they had been summoned.

I began the session by asking, "Why are you here?"

One of them replied, "*For a sovereign country.*"

Another said, "We want an independent nation."

Someone else added, "To preserve our ethnic identity."

I nodded, listening to each of them carefully. It was a completely different experience; elsewhere, people usually ask for peace in relationships, transfers, or good health. But here, these young men were already thinking beyond themselves; their concerns were vast, collective, rooted in identity and belonging.

They were already in the *big mind.*

Gurudev often says, *"We can learn commitment from the insurgents."*

I asked, "What bothers you?"

One by one, they answered:

"We will fight till our last breath."

"We've taken up arms and won't lay them down until our mission is accomplished."

"We're away from our families and won't return until the movement succeeds."

"I want revenge on the army for my brother."

Each reply carried the same fierce, single-minded resolve... a willingness to sacrifice everything for the cause.

My final question was, "What do you expect from this Art of Living program?"

The answers came all at once, a flood of honest voices.

"We hope Gurudev will solve our problems."

"We want to feel real peace within."

"We want Gurudev to help us in creating our own country."

"Our leaders have already met Gurudev; we want to meet him too."

The group was fully engaged, responding with curiosity and trust. I could sense their sincerity; they already knew that I had come as Gurudev's emissary.

As the program progressed, I introduced them to the Sudarshan Kriya. They participated with complete sincerity, with 100 per cent involvement. When they opened their eyes, something had shifted. A quiet stillness filled the room. Some had tears rolling down their cheeks, some spoke of a divine fragrance in the air, and a few sat silently, their throats choking with emotion. I knew then—the Master had worked his magic.

DNLA team learning Sudarshan Kriya.

The fatigue from their long travels had completely melted away. Their faces glowed with calmness and clarity; they had touched a beautiful, peaceful state of mind. Later, I spent personal time with many of them; they dropped all hesitation, speaking freely and openly. They treated me not as an outsider, but as a friend and well-wisher.

By the end, they were eager and excited to experience the Sudarshan Kriya again.

I returned to the forest guesthouse and walked into the small kitchen. A young boy was trying to cook something, but it was clear he had no idea what he was doing. So, I managed with a few bananas for breakfast.

By lunchtime, hunger caught up with me. I went back to the kitchen, thinking I'd prepare something myself. But when I picked up the knife, I paused; it wasn't an ordinary one; it was a heavy meat cutter fixed on a wooden log. I smiled to myself, dropped the idea of cooking, and returned to my faithful bananas... my best friends of the day.

By four in the evening, darkness had already descended over the forest.

That night, Gurudev appeared in my dream. He looked at me with his familiar gentleness and said, "You take care of them." I nodded silently. Then he smiled and added, "You also eat," before fading into light. I woke up with a full heart despite an empty stomach—Gurudev knew I was hungry.

The next morning, I returned to the boot camp. All the participants were already there, waiting eagerly. We continued the program, and once again, everyone had deeply healing and touching experiences.

Later, I connected personally with a few cadres. They shared that they were engineers, coming from good families; yet here they were, living in the jungles and fighting for an independent nation. Their intensity and enthusiasm for their cause were remarkable. I wondered where such unwavering inspiration came from. They reminded me of *Karma Yogis*—fully committed to action; perhaps all they needed was a change in direction, a new purpose for their passion.

When I returned to the guesthouse, I cleaned the entire kitchen, cooked some rice, and found a few radishes to go with it. That became my simple routine for the next few days... quiet service, simple meals, and deep reflection.

One evening, as I was walking near the camp, our ashram's road contractor spotted me. His eyes widened in surprise. "Sir! What are you doing here?" he asked.

I smiled and replied calmly, "I've come here to conduct a program."

He hesitated for a moment, then said quickly, "Sir, *aapka kaam ho jayega* (Your work will be done)," and without another word, he left in haste. I didn't think much of it then, but to my surprise, from that day onward, the road work at the ashram never stopped again. Perhaps he was worried I might complain about him to the DNLA!

We soon concluded the program, and in the end, everyone had a truly profound and uplifting experience. The transformation in their faces, from hardness to peace, said it all.

It was now a time for self-reflection, for them to look within. One by one, they began sharing their experiences.

"The peace we were searching for outside," someone said, "is nothing compared to the peace we have experienced here."

Another added softly, "This is real peace."

A wave of understanding seemed to pass through them; a time of transformation had begun, and the seeds of a new future were quietly sown. Their reverence and faith in Gurudev had deepened beyond measure.

Before leaving, we took a group picture together. They asked me to return soon. There was a special feeling in the air…they felt heard, understood and touched by something greater than words.

As I looked back on those days in the jungle, I realized that something profound had unfolded, not just for them, but within me too. It was a journey where conflict met compassion, and where silence spoke louder than any words.

That was exactly what I had witnessed…not rebels, but wounded hearts longing to be heard. And through Gurudev's grace, even in the midst of the wilderness, they had felt that healing touch.

In that silence of the forest, surrounded by those who once lived by the gun, I felt that presence…tender, watchful, and infinite.

There was a buzzing atmosphere of love, enthusiasm, surrender, and a deep space for peace. Gurudev's wisdom was now reverberating through the entire boot camp.

A group picture with DNLA meditators.

I came back from the camp and slept for the next two days at our ashram. A deep cleansing had happened through the Sudarshan Kriya, and I needed rest to rejuvenate myself. I had no clue what was next, but my heart was full...grateful that they had experienced Gurudev's wisdom.

It was humbling to see how joy could thrive even amidst minimal resources. Their evident inclination to find peace in Gurudev's presence was heart-touching. A world without violence is indeed a dream worth every effort.

A few days later, I received a call from Gurudev's secretariat. "Gurudev is sending a few jackets to you," said the voice on the other end. Before I could ask anything more, the call got disconnected.

Three days later, to my surprise, we received 300 jackets. I immediately called Etika and Longki; they came and distributed the jackets among their team. Their joy knew no bounds, and my heart was filled with happiness watching them wrapped in warmth and gratitude.

The Art of Living
@ArtofLiving

Inspired by Gurudev Sri Sri Ravi Shankar, 300 jackets were given to Ex UPLA and DNLA cadres as part of a Rehabilitation program. Most of them live in jungles, in their boot camps in difficult terrains in the interiors of Karbi Anglong & Dima Hassao of Assam.

3:57 PM · Jan 7, 2023 · **4,333** Views

UPLA and DNLA with jackets.

That winter was one of the coldest in recent times, yet the air was warmer than ever, filled with the grace and compassion of the Master.

What triggered this sudden instruction from Gurudev's secretariat?

There was a prayerful connection between the Master and his militant devotees, an invisible thread of longing and grace. Their hearts had opened in surrender, and their prayers were silently answered. The Master had felt their devotion; his compassion was already in action, and it was bound to be executed.

Gurudev says, *"Devotion brings a healing touch to life. Devotion and faith are the very core of true prayer. In devotion, longing arises, and when longing arises, true prayer happens by itself."*

After the inner healing through Sudarshan Kriya, came the outer protection...the warmth of the jackets shielding them from the cold. A small gesture from the Divine brought immense security and comfort. And what was most touching was, this had happened without anyone asking for it. It was purely an execution of heartfelt prayers. In my experience, every sincere prayer is answered...not always in words, but through silent acts of grace. And so it is for every devotee of Gurudev.

As I look back, the journey to the DNLA camp was not just an outreach; it was a pilgrimage of faith. What began with apprehension and silence unfolded into trust, connection, and a deep awakening. The same hearts once filled with rebellion and resistance had tasted peace through the Master's grace. Gurudev's unseen hand moved through every moment...from the dense jungles to the warmth of the jackets, from silence to surrender.

Each experience reaffirmed that transformation is not born out of force, but from understanding; not through fear, but through love. When hearts open to the higher truth, even the toughest souls melt into compassion. Gurudev's vision of a world free from violence isn't a distant dream. It is unfolding, one healed heart at a time.

The roads in the ashram were nearly complete, but a far deeper path—the path of love—had been laid in the boot camp.

9

Panch Kilo

Before a need could even fully arise, it somehow got taken care of...

One evening, I was standing on the main road, about 100 meters from the Diphu ashram, waiting for an auto rickshaw. Usually they come every 10–15 minutes, but that day, I kept waiting... ten minutes, twenty, thirty. Almost forty-five minutes passed.

In the early days, there was hardly any transport around, so we depended completely on public autos.

But standing there on that quiet road, watching the light change, it almost felt meditative. I wasn't stressed. A few times I had even walked all the way to town when no auto came by, so this long wait felt normal, even peaceful.

Gurudev says, "Prayer is a vital tool to improve your life. When the obstacle feels too much to handle, deep prayer can work miracles. What you can do, you do. What you cannot do, you pray for it. Whatever you do, remember that a higher power has the final say, and you can tap into that power through your prayers."

Across the road stood an old, broken structure. Something about it kept pulling my attention. After waiting for so long, I felt the urge to go and see what it is. I crossed the road, pushed the door gently, and the whole thing gave way, it was that weak.

Inside, to my surprise, was a Shiva temple. Silent, covered in cobwebs and dust, but still beautiful. A forgotten space.

The next day was Gandhi Jayanti, and the thought came immediately: we should clean this place. A small seva. A small beginning.

That night when I returned, around twenty local kids were hanging around the ashram. They often came for food, *satsang*, to play, or simply to feel safe. Our ashram used to be called a *bhoot bangla* by the villagers, but over time, as people started visiting, that old fear just disappeared. The space became a kind of shelter, a place to breathe, sit and relax.

The next morning, we gathered a team of about 25 people, including our ashramites, and walked to the abandoned Shiva temple. Everyone came with full enthusiasm. One of the boys, Ganesh, climbed right up to the top and started sweeping the roof. As we cleaned, we found an inscription: the temple had been established in 1975.

I was coordinating the group when suddenly a man from the village arrived, asking for Ganesh. I asked his name and he replied, "Shankar. I'm Ganesh's father. I've been looking for him."

The son was named Ganesh (Bhagawan Shiva's son), and the father was named Shankar (another name of Bhagawan Shiva)! It felt as if the cosmic divinity was displaying its comic sense too!

I asked him, almost casually, "Whose temple is this?"

He replied, "It's a Shiva temple… and I'm the priest here."

I asked him why the temple had been left in such a poor state. His face changed immediately. It became heavy, almost helpless.

He said softly, "The owner of the land never allowed anyone to do puja here."

I asked about the owner.

He replied, "He was unwell ... and he passed away yesterday evening."

For a moment, I just stood there. I had crossed that road countless times, but only *last evening* did something pull my attention toward that broken structure. It felt like a call from the divine, a way to protect the temple before any confusion or conflict could arise.

By the same evening, after we finished cleaning, the temple doors were open again. Devotees from nearby villages came on their own. They lit earthen lamps. Someone arranged a small electric connection. The space came alive, as if it had been waiting for this moment.

Later, Shankar told me, "This is a *panch-kilo* Shiva temple." I was soon to find out the significance of the "panch-kilo" epithet.

After years of silence, it was functional again, a living place of worship for the community.

A little ahead of the ashram, inside the prison grounds, there is another Shiva temple, the six-kilo Shiva temple. Every time I went there to conduct the Prison SMART program, I would first offer water to the Shivlinga. It became a small routine, a moment of silence before the sessions.

Two days after we cleaned the panch-kilo temple, something interesting happened. On the same main road, just towards the city, someone, maybe inspired by the seva, renovated the four-kilo Shiva temple. Suddenly, the pattern became clear.

The railway station, where the city begins, has a Shiva temple. Then, almost after every kilometer, there is a one-kilo, two-kilo, three-kilo temple. The panch-kilo was the only missing link. Later, I came to know that this alignment continues up tol 12 kilometers, one Shiva temple after another.

That evening still feels unbelievable to me. As if a puzzle was quietly falling into place. Our ashram's Shiva temple was the missing dot in this entire chain.

It felt like a cosmic plan, the quiet effect of the *sadhana* happening in the ashram seemed to be slowly spreading through the region.

One afternoon, I was doing my usual work when Samir ji called.

He said, "Champion, get groceries for the ashram. There is a high probability of a lockdown."

I had no idea what he was talking about, but coincidentally, I was planning to go out and buy provisions anyway. The weather was calm, the afternoon felt normal, and I stepped outside to interact with a few neighbors.

As I walked from house to house, I asked everyone, "Are you aware there might be a lockdown?"

Most people just laughed. They had no clue. Life was running as usual.

I visited a few nearby homes to check on their well-being. Many houses were wide open but empty; the adults had gone out for daily wage work. A few children took me around and showed me their small bamboo kitchens. Most of them barely had any groceries. Many families lived on a simple rule: *earn today, eat today.*

Gurudev says, "For human rights to flourish, human values must be nurtured, just as the roots of a tree must be watered for the fruit to grow."

So that evening, I opened my phone and made a list of 32 families who needed help. Then I went to the market to buy groceries.

Panch-kilo rice for 32 people meant 160 kilos, plus our regular ashram expenses. We stocked up on whatever we could and told everyone, "Come to the ashram tomorrow."

The very next day, 22 March 2020, the lockdown was declared. No movement. Everyone had to stay where they were. We had been watching the news about the corona virus, but none of us imagined it would affect the interiors of the Northeast so suddenly.

Still, it was a precaution from the government, and people were confused, uncertain and worried.

The next morning, when we opened the ashram gate, there were 260 women waiting.

Two hundred and sixty.

They didn't know exactly what we would do, but they had come with hope.

We took down everyone's names and started distributing. Panch-kilo rice for around 50 families, whatever we could manage with the supplies we had.

It was the first morning of lockdown, and already, the scale of the need was in front of us.

Those who didn't receive rice that day tried to hide their disappointment, but you could see it in their eyes. I told them gently, "Come tomorrow, we will arrange it."

That evening, I called Vishal ji and explained that we needed funds urgently for rice. He didn't ask a single question. He simply sent the money. With that, we bought enough supplies for 250 families for the next day.

But the next morning, nearly 400 people were waiting.

In those days, our ashram had no gate, no boundary. Anyone could walk straight in. I took a quick video on my phone while we were distributing, and shared it with a few of my students.

Panch-kilo rice distribution.

The moment that video reached them, funds started arriving, enough for another 500 families. I told the crowd, "Please come tomorrow, we will distribute again."

And this went on for nearly ten days! Grace was flowing, and it was apparent.

By then, Gurudev had started the daily noon meditation sessions. That became our rhythm: Morning *sadhana*. Then, rice distribution. Packing up everything before lunch. Serving with an open heart.

Our team built simple systems, best practices, a flow… and we were genuinely happy doing this seva. Every day felt meaningful, disciplined and graceful, even in the middle of uncertainty.

Every day, around 250–400 people would come. We managed queues, distributed rice, and the villagers would bow down, offering their pranams to Gurudev. I kept recording short videos and sending them to our people.

Magically, the funds for the next day would always come in advance. By evening, the rice for the following day was already ordered and delivered.

My day was full: online meditation classes, morning *sadhana,* then *seva,* and in the evening meditating again with Gurudev and watching *Ramayan* (a popular TV serial that was being replayed in those days).

It truly felt like Gurudev's blessing of Annapurna in action, unfolding at the perfect time, embracing so many people through one simple act of rice distribution.

One fine morning, a huge crowd gathered again. But that day we had very limited rice.

By 11:55 a.m., our stock was completely over. Almost 200 women were still waiting in the queue.

You could feel their helplessness. Not a single person complained. No one argued.

They simply stood there, quiet, holding their hope inside.

We were sensitive, but we also had to be practical. I told the ladies gently, "The stock is over for today."

At the same moment, I checked my phone, we were waiting to begin the noon meditation with Gurudev.

A message arrived. Funds had just come. Immediately, I ordered the next stock of rice and sat down for meditation. When we opened our eyes after the session, the new bags had already arrived. We continued the distribution.

It genuinely felt as if we had a direct tie-up with Annapurna Devi.

One need would arise, and before the thought even settled, the help would come.

Meanwhile, COVID was spreading deeper. Phase 2 was followed by Phase 3; the situation was getting worse. Many villagers were fully dependent on the ashram. They would break the queue despite repeated requests, simply out of fear that they might return home empty-handed.

Pregnant women, women on their menstrual cycles, and mothers carrying small babies would walk 7–8 kilometers to reach us.

We restricted distribution to women only because they truly understood the value of food, and they would prioritize their families.

By then, the COVID situation had become extremely severe across the country.

One day, Karthik ji suggested that we explore the possibility of converting our ashram into a COVID Care Centre.

Around that time, even our own ashramites—Augustine and Kamal—had been infected. They told us about the terrible conditions in the local COVID centre. There was fear, confusion, and almost no proper care. When they returned to the ashram, it became clear that the situation outside was collapsing.

The decision was on me.

That night, after watching *Ramayan* together, I asked the group, "Should we convert our ashram into a COVID Care Centre?"

Everyone replied, "As Gurudev wishes."

I said, "Jiyenge to saath jiyenge."

They answered, "Marenge to saath marenge."

I told them, "We are not here to die. We are here to help others live."

The next morning, I drafted a proposal and went to meet Deputy Commissioner Chandradhwajh Singha, at the DC Office. The staff at the entrance were reluctant, but they had seen me many times before, coming for different programs and permissions. Eventually, they allowed me in.

I presented the proposal, explaining our readiness to convert the ashram into a COVID Care Centre. The DC listened quietly, and then his expression softened. He said, "GOD has sent you."

Without wasting even a minute, he asked me to join him. He took me in his car, and we drove straight to the ashram for an immediate survey.

We planned a 30-bed COVID Care Centre, which could be expanded to a 100-bed dormitory if needed. The deputy commissioner immediately approved it and instructed the medical team to prepare. My responsibility was to arrange PPE kits, oxygen concentrators, and all essential materials.

We shifted ourselves to the other side of the ashram with minimal resources.

The ashram was now officially going to become a COVID Care Centre.

But the DC's car entering the ashram created suspicion in the village. By evening, word had spread everywhere. As happens with mob psychology, people gathered one by one, until the entire place was surrounded.

Their message was clear:

"We cannot let this place become a COVID centre."

They were angry, insecure and frightened.

The moment I stepped out, the crowd closed in.

Women came forward, speaking over each other, "This place can never become a COVID care centre."

I tried explaining calmly, but fear does not listen to logic.

I was surrounded by nearly a hundred women: emotional, protective, worried about their families, their children, their village.

I stood there quietly for a moment, letting them speak. Their fear was genuine. They weren't opposing us out of anger; they were scared that bringing COVID patients close to the village would put their families at risk.

I listened first.

Only after that, I spoke.

I said, "I understand your fear. But people are dying because there is no proper care. If we don't help now, who will? Gurudev has always taught us to serve when service is needed the most."

But they weren't ready.

Some women started crying.

Some raised their voices.

Some begged me not to go ahead.

At that moment, I felt two forces pulling inside me: my duty to serve, and my responsibility to protect the trust of the villagers who had grown close to the ashram.

Slowly, a few elders arrived. They tried to calm the crowd, but emotions were running high.

One lady came forward and said, "If anything happens to our children, who will take responsibility?"

Another said, "We come here because this place feels safe. Don't take that away."

Their words carried pain, not hostility.

So I didn't argue. I didn't push.

They were not letting me convince them.

They respected me, but the unknown fear was stronger: *what if the virus spreads to their homes?*

In that panic, they forgot that the ashram had been feeding them for days. They didn't see that this COVID Centre was our Plan B, in case the situation collapsed and lives needed to be saved locally.

No one was ready to listen. Voices rose. The shouting grew louder.

I don't know what happened inside me at that moment. I closed my eyes and prayed to Gurudev for strength. When I opened them, something shifted. I felt something rise inside me: A courage that wasn't mine, an unknown valor.

With a firm, lion-like voice, I said, "Whatever you want to do, do. But we will make this a COVID Care centre."

They were shocked. The sudden strength in my voice had unsettled them.

Slowly, they stepped back. The crowd dispersed.

The path ahead was clear now.

We prepared everything: beds, equipment, systems. We had one prayer in our hearts: *Let this facility be ready, but let it never be needed.*

It was our shield, our Plan B, created with *seva* and faith.

Karthik ji immediately stepped in. Through IAHV, he arranged four oxygen concentrators for us. We managed to raise funds for oximeters, PPE kits, and whatever else was required.

Slowly, piece by piece, the readiness for a COVID Care Centre started taking shape.

The centre was inaugurated by Honourable Member of Parliament Horensing Bey. When he saw the effort, he had tears in his eyes. He said it was a blessing from Gurudev; that in such a remote place, an ashram was standing ready to save lives.

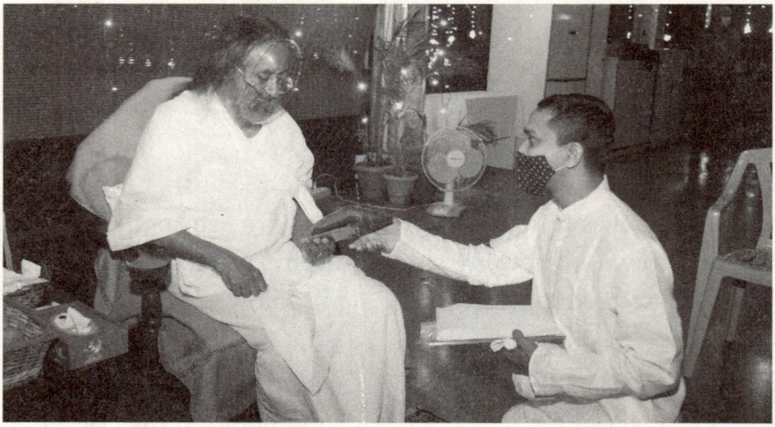

Sharing updates about the Covid Care Centre with Gurudev.

I shifted to a temporary structure inside the ashram, which was originally being built as Gurudev's kutir. Our ashramites moved to Gate No. 3.

We lived with minimal facilities, but no one complained. Everyone's mind was on seva.

For the next four months, our routine remained the same: distributing panch-kilo bags of rice, managing the queues; attending two meditations with Gurudev each day; and watching the *Ramayan* in the evenings.

Life was simple. Disciplined. Sacred. And completely devoted to service.

In those days, I often wondered: *What is the truth of life?*

Everything around us was uncertain; people were scared, situations kept changing, and the world felt fragile. Yet inside, there is something that never changes. Something that doesn't disappear, doesn't break, doesn't perish.

Something eternal.

And when we pay attention to that inner element, a different kind of strength rises in us: the strength to face whatever is happening outside.

Gurudev says, "When the mind is broken, when the heart is shaken from within, a person becomes powerless. Inner strength comes through meditation, through knowledge, through knowing the truth of life. A strong mind can carry a weak body. But a weak mind cannot carry even a strong body."

In the middle of the pandemic, these words felt more real than ever.

One day, a lady was carrying her sack of rice down the steps. She looked unwell, a little weak. Suddenly, she slipped, fell, and the entire sack of rice spilled onto the dusty road.

Without saying a word, she got on her knees and began picking up every grain, one handful at a time.

Watching her, all of us stood silent.

It was a very emotional moment.

In that instant, we felt profoundly grateful... grateful that we were on the giving side and not the receiving side; grateful that we had the capacity, the health, and the blessing to serve.

Trying times bring out our ability to endure, to adapt, to become stronger, kinder, and wiser.

The second COVID wave was a test, not only for health systems, but for humanity itself.

This was the moment to invoke the valor inside us, to stand together, and to rise again.

The temporary building where I stayed had no windows. The nights were extremely cold. Eventually, I also moved to Gate No. 3 and stayed with Jirsong. We shared the same small space.

One day, without my knowledge, Jirsong tested positive for COVID.

We were living together—the same room, the same air; but I did not get infected. Not once.

It felt as if some higher power was protecting me, carrying me through each day. I was teaching, serving, meditating, and doing seva at our Panch Kilo Ashram with complete surrender.

Looking back, I can only call it Gurudev's grace, nothing else.

Eventually, winter arrived. The cold was harsh, especially for villagers who had already suffered so much during the lockdown. We raised funds and procured a thousand good-quality blankets under Project Blanket of Grace in November 2020.

After rice, people now felt the warmth of Gurudev's love through those blankets.

Every now and then, you would see a small group of women walking towards the Panch Kilo Ashram—laughing, chatting, carrying their worries and hopes, just to experience that same love and reassurance.

COVID eventually faded, but the memories of care from Gurudev's ashram remained etched in the hearts of more than a thousand families. For them, Panch Kilo was no longer merely an ashram; it had become a sanctuary: a space of protection, belonging and grace.

Seva was no longer something we *did*. It had become who we were.

Our lifestyle. Our rhythm. Our very way of breathing.

New initiatives began to unfold naturally, one after another: stitching classes empowering women with dignity and skill; warm sweaters reaching families during the harsh winter months; organic farming training restoring both soil and self-reliance; Project Blanket of Grace 2.0 spreading comfort; solar lights illuminating homes that had long known darkness;

Project Fluoride Nilogon bringing healthier water; and disaster-relief efforts extending help wherever it was needed.

Each project sent gentle ripples through the community. What began as relief work slowly turned into relationships. From cautious conversations grew trust. From trust blossomed connections. And from connections emerged a shared sense of family.

The ashram grew vibrant, alive with movement, laughter, prayer and purpose. People no longer came only for assistance; they came to belong. They came to share their joys and struggles. They came because something sacred had taken root there.

Looking back, it was never about rice, blankets, or solar lights. It was about love finding expression through service. What began as a response to the crisis had become a living example of grace in action.

And in serving them, quietly and humbly, we discovered that we ourselves were being transformed.

Even today, Panch Kilo reminds me of what Gurudev often says: *"Remember, life is short. While you are on earth, do some good work, bring happiness, and turn tears into smiles."*

Briefing Gurudev about our service projects during Covid.

10

64 Bighas

From forgotten soil to sacred space—grace did it all.

In my initial days at Diphu, the then Principal Secretary Smt Jayashree Daulaguphu's son participated in the Art of Living program. While the program was underway, she invited Longbir ji and me for breakfast. Overwhelmed by her son's experience, she told Longbir ji to collect the allotment letter for a piece of land for the Art of Living. I had no idea any such possibility even existed.

A few days later, I received a call from Deepak ji (a senior Art of Living teacher). He told me that I should stop travelling, stay in one place, and continue the Art of Living activities from Diphu. I had a difference of opinion; just sitting in Diphu without wider engagement didn't make much sense to me.

Deepak ji then checked directly with Gurudev: "Gurudev, a piece of land has been allotted and Vishnu Prakash is conducting programs there. Can he take care of the land?"

Gurudev responded with a simple, affirmative "Yes."

Deepak ji sent me the screenshot of Gurudev's message, and I accepted the project as prasad, with complete surrender.

The facility allotted to us was an unfinished structure standing isolated in a forest, which was once meant to be a tourist complex set up by the Karbi Anglong Autonomous Council.

In the beginning, I stayed at Longbir ji's house. They cared for me like their own family. But one day, a strong feeling arose within me—that I must stay on the allotted land itself. All our well-wishers and local devotees cautioned me against it, insisting it wasn't safe or practical. But I was determined.

One evening, I simply picked up my belongings and went there with Sonasing, our organic farming master trainer. That was the beginning of a new chapter.

The place was completely ransacked—it looked like a *bhoot bungalow (haunted house)*. The half-constructed buildings stood abandoned, everything was covered in soot and patches of black paint. There was no power, no water, and not even a toilet. It was an old, abandoned tourist complex.

By evening, the entire area fell silent. Sonasing had to leave to take care of his cows. Before he left, we did Guru Pooja together, and thankfully we had carried some food with us.

I prepared a makeshift bed in the open, on top of the meditation hall. From there, I watched the sunset fade slowly and the night gently take over the sky. By around eight in the evening, I fell asleep... deep, unbroken, like an N3 sleep.

Suddenly, around 10 p.m., a terrifying sound started echoing from multiple directions.

"Geko... geko... geko..."

At first, I tried covering myself with a thin blanket, hoping it would calm my nerves, but the sound only grew louder and more intense.

Alone, in the middle of the night, in a jungle, without electricity, in complete darkness—it was the most frightening sound I had ever experienced. Sleep was impossible. And there was no way to go back.

Around 11 p.m., to my surprise, Longbir ji arrived searching for me. He had heard that I was staying alone in the ashram and had immediately come looking. Seeing him, I felt an immense sense of relief wash over me. He had brought a solar lantern and a bed.

Both of us were exhausted, so we simply slept on the terrace. Strangely, the *geko* sound vanished the moment he arrived.

At dawn, we hurried back to Longbir ji's house to freshen up.

That first night became the ice-breaker for the ashram, and a silent confirmation that yes, we *could* survive there. Soon after, the trust sanctioned a small budget for basic living requirements. Gradually, a few of my YLTP students expressed their willingness to step out of their villages and build a livelihood. Augustine and Jirsong arrived first, followed by Kamal ji, and together they became the first team of our little ashram family.

We managed water from a nearby house, gathered firewood, and arranged a few basic utensils for cooking. Eventually, we discovered an old ring well inside the ashram premises itself. We later connected electricity through a transformer next to the land.

With some tarpaulin sheets, a bit of groceries, a few solar lights, and absolutely no fixed idea of what we were "supposed" to do, we simply began. Over the next month, the ashram slowly became more approachable. We cleared the jungle-like growth, arranged a couple of cylinders, gathered more utensils, set up a proper connection from the ring well, and managed with electricity that came and went unpredictably.

I continued travelling for programs, while the boys stayed back and took care of the ashram. Together, step by step, we were breathing life into a place that had once felt abandoned.

From day one, we began with a simple routine: morning *sadhana, seva,* and evening *satsang*. Those three pillars became the heartbeat of the ashram. We had a beautiful picture of Gurudev, a sofa someone had donated, and a few daris spread across the hall. That was enough to feel his presence.

I continued travelling, conducting programs and bringing people back to the ashram so they could experience the space we were slowly nurturing.

On the last day of the Happiness Program, a group from Lumding visited us. Their joy and enthusiasm filled the space with new energy. Soon after, in 2017, we celebrated Gurudev's birthday at the ashram, just after completing a YLTP program. That celebration marked a turning point.

Slowly, gradually, almost silently, the place started transforming... day by day, breath by breath. What once felt abandoned was now coming alive with laughter, devotion and purpose.

I used to sleep in the Hemphu hall, and one night, it began raining very heavily. As usual, I lay down to sleep, expecting nothing unusual. But that night, the rain was relentless. The entire hall started to flood, water rising almost to where I was sleeping. I kept waiting for the night to somehow pass so we could add more tarpaulin near the windows in the morning.

To my shock, I noticed a snake lying quietly right next to me. It wasn't moving—just silently watching me. And I was equally helpless, staring back at it. There we were, both stranded by the rain, waiting for the downpour to stop!

In that moment, I remembered Gurudev's words during one of our travels: *"With me, your life is like the life of Pi."*

Except, instead of encountering a Bengal Tiger, I had a snake for company... both of us drenched, tired, and stuck in the same situation.

I simply surrendered. A thought came: Lord *Vishnu also rests on a snake.*

With that, I closed my eyes and actually slept.

By morning, the rain had stopped, the sky had cleared, and the snake had quietly disappeared. We got up, cleaned the place, and began preparing for the upcoming YLTP program.

Every course we conducted transformed people—and in turn, transformed the ashram. Someone would come forward for physical seva, another would donate something essential, and slowly we built the ashram, brick by brick, each project with its own timeline and quality.

One fine day, I made a simple list of the items we needed and mapped around ten devotees to different aspects of basic infrastructure development. I invited all of them to the ashram.

What happened that day was nothing short of magical.

I would take each devotee around the premises, and they would spontaneously say, "Vishnu ji, I want to contribute to this specific work in the ashram."

Then I would show them the letter I had prepared—already listing exactly the same items they had chosen. It felt as if the divine plan had been written long before, and we were merely playing our parts in a drama already directed.

The local devotees were left stunned, witnessing how perfectly everything aligned. Usually, people commit and then forget or delay, but this time, seeing the divine synchronicity on paper, everyone worked sincerely and immediately.

One devotee offered to renovate the Hemphu hall windows, so we could finally sleep without water seeping in during the rains. And just like that, one improvement led to another.

The ashram had begun to grow—slowly, steady, and full of his grace. Programs were happening back-to-back, and the energy of the place was growing day by day.

One day, while I was conducting a meditation session, a group of people suddenly arrived, looking for me. Without any warning, they began shouting and abusing me loudly. My heart started pounding... they were furious, their anger almost explosive. They threatened the workers, demanding that all work be stopped immediately. They even began throwing small things around, insisting that we vacate the place at once.

Within moments, Longbir ji and Mohan ji rushed in. They started speaking to the group in the local language. The atmosphere was tense, the air felt heavy, and the situation could turn either way.

Around that time, nearly 24-plus local organizations had developed a misunderstanding: that the Art of Living, an external NGO from Bengaluru, was attempting to take over tribal land. The rumour had spread quickly, and the situation had escalated. The group that confronted us was unwilling to listen; their anger kept rising. They continued abusing and threatening us.

Within minutes, all the laborers fled in fear. Only Longbir ji and Mohan ji stood their ground, facing an aggressive mob of more than fifty people. The matter had turned so sensitive that we were left with no option but to seek police assistance.

By the next morning, social media was flooded with headlines: "Art of Living grabbing tribal land."

Some posts even went to the extreme of claiming that Gurudev himself was eyeing tribal land, a completely baseless and hurtful accusation.

I asked Longbir ji, "But we already have the allotment from the Karbi Anglong Autonomous Council, right?"

He replied calmly, "It's just an allotment. We still need to register the land." That was the beginning of a long and painful struggle.

We were instructed to do no development, no construction, and only very limited activities. Threats began pouring in, mostly directed towards Longbir ji and Mohan ji. They would stand in front of me like shields, absorbing the anger and abuses coming our way. No one was willing to listen. The issue had become a topic of heated discussion everywhere.

We were labeled as converters, accused of false intentions, and multiple baseless litigations surfaced. I was also under constant threat. One day, Longbir ji came to me visibly shaken and angry. He said, "The local community has warned that we will be outcast from our tribe if we continue supporting the Art of Living."

Despite that, both he and Mohan ji stood like lions: brave, steady, and ready to face humiliation, abuses and threats with unwavering courage.

This continued for several weeks. We were stuck; we couldn't pack up, and we couldn't walk away. Every day I would look at Gurudev's message: "Vishnu Prakash can take care of the ashram."

I was clueless... helpless... but that one line kept me rooted.

We continued with our *sadhana* and *satsang,* and with renewed commitment, we started our service activities again. Even in the storm, devotion became our anchor.

We were in a situation where we could neither swallow nor spit it out, like a snake struggling to gulp an Indian shrew (*chachundar*). Yet we continued with our programs, sadhana, and satsang, holding on to whatever strength we could find. Pressure was coming from every corner, and finally, in complete helplessness, I travelled to Bengaluru to seek Gurudev's guidance.

I took an appointment, and Gurudev called me to Shakti Kutir. As I began narrating the situation…what felt like the most severe challenge of my life…Gurudev listened silently, while pacing to and fro inside the Kutir as he often does.

When I finished pouring my heart out, He simply said, "It will be done. You be in touch with them."

Just those few words: light, effortless, yet full of certainty.

Then he handed me a box of Swiss chocolates.

I left Shakti Kutir with a smile, carrying renewed strength, renewed commitment…and that unmistakable feeling that everything would unfold exactly as he intended.

With newfound determination, Longbir ji, Mohan ji, and I ran from pillar to post. We met every section of society—organizations, community leaders, bureaucrats, and politicians. What happened next was nothing short of magical. Each conversation, each visit, felt like a small step carved by his grace.

Eventually, we met the member of Parliament who had come to inaugurate the Fluoride Nilogon project. After listening to us, he assured, "It will be done." That assurance felt like a door opening.

Once Gurudev had blessed the situation, it truly became only a matter of time.

And exactly one year later, in September 2020, the Karbi Anglong Autonomous Council passed a resolution in their executive meeting:

"64 bighas of land to be allotted to The Art of Living."

The Master's words carry a voltage of their own. Once spoken, the entire subtle universe begins moving to fulfiLl them.

A council member came to Bengaluru and offered the allotment letter to Gurudev. But to my surprise, the letter mentioned only 20 bighas. They assured me that another letter for the remaining land would be issued soon. I felt the work was almost over, but Gurudev once again reminded me, "Be in touch with them."

KAAC members presenting registration letter to Gurudev.

Gurudev often says, *"Feeling and experiencing infinity within the finite body, living timelessly within the span of life... this is what you are here for."*

And once again, life was preparing to show exactly that.

Around the same time, the Union Cabinet requested Gurudev's help in acquiring land in Bengaluru for a Karbi Bhawan, a cultural home for the Karbi community. In his boundless compassion, Gurudev even offered space within the Bengaluru Ashram itself. But the ministers desired a separate land somewhere in the city.

With Gurudev's blessings, a devotee came forward, wishing to sell their plot. Gurudev connected them directly with the council. It turned out to be a perfect match...a divine alignment, a win-win situation for everyone.

Eventually, two plots were registered in the name of the Karbi Anglong Autonomous Council near the Bengaluru Airport for Karbi Bhawan. Celebrations followed; news articles everywhere spoke of how a saint helped a tribal community acquire land in Bengaluru.

It took us another two years to secure the remaining 44 bighas. Every day, Longbir ji, Mohan ji, and I would visit one office after another: ministers, secretaries, revenue officials. It became our daily routine. I would leave after breakfast, never knowing what time I would return. Eventually, I began carrying my lunch with me, because some days stretched endlessly. This continued for several months.

And then, *Satyameva Jayate.*

The council finally passed the resolution and permanently allotted the entire land to The Art of Living.

Member of Parliament Sh Horen Sing Bey receiving Gurudev's blessings.

It was a victory of trust, a victory of service, and above all, it was a manifestation of the Master's *sankalpa*. His words had moved through people, systems, and the unseen layers of existence to fulfill itself.

We became the first organization to be officially invited and given a proper setup to serve the people of the region. It was not just land, it was an opportunity to touch lives, uplift communities, and honor the spirit of Karbi Anglong.

The initial days at the ashram were extremely challenging. However, everything began to shift after we organized an Advanced Program with Dinesh Ghodke, during which he shared a story that has remained etched in my heart ever since.

One evening, Gurudev was walking along the banks of the Ganga in Rishikesh. Holding Dinesh's hand, he asked, *"Who do you think earns the most punya (merit) here?"*

Someone replied, *"Those who take a bath in the Ganga."*

Gurudev smiled and said, *"After taking a bath, people need to change their clothes, find a safe place to keep their belongings, eat food, and rest. Look at the small inns and houses near the ghats. Those who stand there and make it convenient for others earn the greatest merit, because they support a devotee's journey."*

This insight was deeply moving. It helped me understand the true meaning of my work at the ashram. I realized that the Master had chosen me not for visibility, but for service; to create a space where those who cannot travel far could still experience his presence. That understanding gave purpose to every challenge and strengthened my commitment to serve.

Another story shared by Gurudev illustrates a humble and humorous solution to even the most unexpected problems.

One day, a dog began barking outside Bhagawan Ram's court. He demanded justice, but everyone ignored him. The barking grew so loud that it disturbed Bhagawan Ram's sleep, and he was finally brought before the court.

The dog explained that the highway had been built for everyone—elephants, horses and oxen, but not for dogs. Moreover, a merchant had thrown a stone at him while he was walking on the road.

The merchant was summoned to the court. He admitted his actions and was prepared to accept any punishment. The entire court laughed at his behavior, but no one knew how to deliver justice to a dog. Ministers consulted legal texts, but ultimately decided to ask the dog what punishment he wished to impose.

Everyone expected the dog to demand a short imprisonment, a fine, or some minor punishment. To their astonishment, the dog requested that the merchant be appointed as an ashram administrator. The court was shocked. It seemed more like a reward than a punishment.

Lord Ram himself asked the dog if he wanted to reconsider, but the dog remained firm. He explained, *"In my previous life, I was an ashram administrator, and life is far harder than a dog's."*

The entire court burst into laughter.

Gurudev often uses stories like this to resolve complex situations with simplicity, wisdom and humor. This is the beauty of having a master's guidance that teaches through lightness, insight, and joy.

One night, Longbir ji shared a profound thought with me: "If people hate you, they may try to kill you. But if they love you, they will give their lives for you."

Today, the Art of Living is one of the most respected organizations in the region. From World Yoga Day to World

Meditation Day, people from all walks of life come to us, and we have truly become part of the local community.

With the trust's support, we built a boundary wall and continued improving the ashram. Slowly, more and more people began visiting. Every day, the ashram grows—both in facilities and in spirit.

Currently, the ashram has a residential capacity of 100 guests and hosts numerous higher-level programs, including the Advanced Program, Blessings Program, Sanyam Program, and Residential Happiness Program, to name a few. Each program is a step forward in bringing the Master's vision to life.

One day, Longbir ji and I went to meet Gurudev and asked Him, "What should we name this ashram?"

Gurudev smiled and said, "The Art of Living International Center."

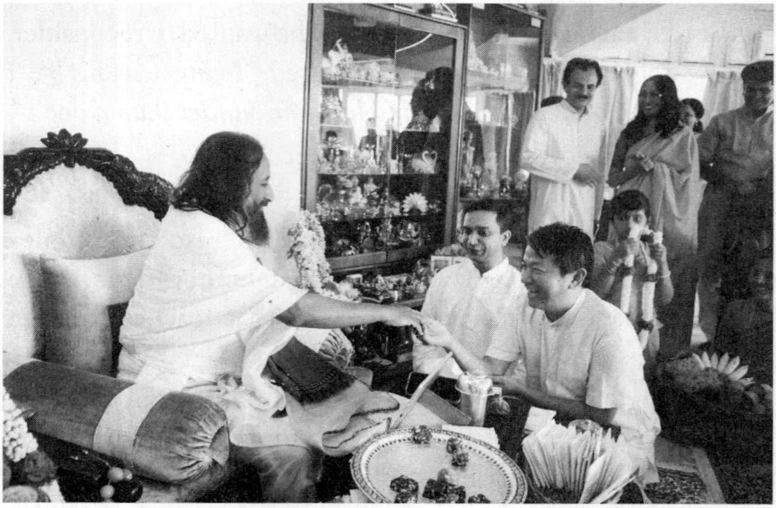

Gurudev blessing Diphu ashram as "The Art of Living International Center."

I immediately handed him an appreciation letter from Michigan University by Dr Louann Palmer who had come to learn the Art of Living program from USA at the Diphu ashram. Gurudev looked at it with quiet amazement and said, "People from all around the world will keep coming."

And indeed, with his blessings, people continue to arrive from across the globe, finding deep solace in their own tribal home—a sanctuary away from home, yet filled with the warmth of his presence.

From its beginnings as a *bhoot bungalow*, the ashram has now become the epicenter of numerous Art of Living projects, uplifting humanity and spreading human values. It is a source of inspiration to thousands, fully blossoming in every sense.

The moment one enters the ashram, they read the words on the gate: "You can bring all your worries, but you cannot take them back."

The ashram is alive with nature and life: rabbits, cows, turtles, royal swans, over 60 varieties of birds, turkeys, slow lorises, geckos, cats, and owls roam freely. It also houses a watchtower, a water filter project serving 135 families across three villages, 21 cottages, a beautiful tree house, a *yagna shala* and a serene abode for Gurudev and Bhanumaa, to name just a few of its wonders.

What began as a humble, abandoned land has now become a vibrant sanctuary—a living testament to devotion, perseverance, and the Master's blessings.

The ashram also preserves the traditional artifacts of the local tribe, celebrating and safeguarding their heritage. Recently, a statue of Ransiga Sarpo was installed.

"Rang Sina Sarpo" (also referred to as *Ru Rangsina Sarpo*) is a legendary Karbi deity who descended from heaven to teach the Karbi people their culture, traditions, and arts. He is regarded as the first mentor of music, art, and culture for the Karbi tribe and is revered for guiding them toward prosperity and well-being. His name is also associated with cultural events, festivals and awards that honor and preserve Karbi heritage.

The moment one enters the ashram, there is a special vibe that lifts away all tiredness and heaviness; a serene, transformative energy that touches every visitor.

It leaves everyone in awe and amazement, a testament to how the Master's *sankalpa* has manifested so beautifully, harmoniously blending landscapes, lakes, and grace. Diphu Ashram is now a beacon of devotion, service, culture, and inspiration—a living testament to how faith, perseverance and divine guidance can transform a dream into reality. And this, truly, is just the beginning.

11

The Interlocutor

In one evening, the burden of years found a place to rest.

During my meditations, the words of Gurudev... *"Take care of them"*... kept echoing in my mind. Again and again. I didn't know what it meant at first or how I was supposed to act on it.

Earlier, I had been to the DNLA boot camp. Their cadres had a beautiful experience learning Sudarshan Kriya. They received love, grace, and even jackets; yet I still felt something was missing, something deeper that we hadn't reached.

One evening, while leading a Happiness Program at our Diphu Ashram, I showed the video *'Sri Sri in the Northeast'*. Towards its end, Gurudev says, *"We will not stop till the last gun is laid down in the region."*

That line kept looping in my mind long after the video ended. It felt like a quiet instruction... or maybe a reminder. And I knew I couldn't ignore it.

For days, that sentence wouldn't leave me. It wasn't dramatic, but it was quiet, steady, like someone gently knocking from inside.

I kept asking myself: *What does "take care of them" actually look like on the ground?* Not in theory. Not in speeches. But in real life, with real people.

Slowly, the answer began showing itself, not in big moments but in small ones: the way the cadres opened up after Kriya, the way they laughed during *satsang*, the way they shared their struggles without hiding behind fear or uniform.

I realized they didn't need more jackets or more programs. They needed someone to just show up and to build trust, brick by brick.

That is when something shifted inside me. My work wasn't about conducting one program and leaving. It was about becoming a presence in their lives, a bridge between who they were and who they could become.

One night during December 2022, while I was having dinner, my phone rang. It was an unknown number. "Vishnu Prakash, where are you?" asked a man. His voice was soft and crisp.

"At the Diphu Ashram," I replied.

"We want to meet you."

The next morning, a group of three men arrived at the ashram. They sat down politely and began asking about my visit to the DNLA boot camp. Their questions were soft, diplomatic, almost casual, but it didn't take me long to realize they were from the central investigating bureau.

They were respectful and humble, yet extremely sharp. They acted as if they knew nothing, but it was clear they already knew a lot. I briefed them on everything: what I had seen, what I had experienced, the conversations I had, and assured them of full cooperation. Whatever information they needed, I provided openly and confidently.

They seemed at ease in the quiet atmosphere of the ashram. Before leaving, they even expressed interest in learning meditation.

Their visits continued in the weeks that followed. Each time, the pattern was the same; a gentle approach on the outside, razor-sharp attention on the inside. They were tracking every detail, even events from two years earlier. I had never seen such professionalism.

For me, it felt like walking on a sword's edge…keeping trust on both sides, the Investigating Bureau and the DNLA, without slipping. Maintaining that balance required focus, clarity and a lot of inner steadiness.

I truly wanted to bring an end to this cat-and-mouse phase. The uncertainty, the questions from every side, the pressure building in the background; it had gone on long enough. One day, I reached out to Mukteshwar ji again and told him that it was time for us to meet Gurudev.

Mukteshwar ji too was under constant investigation and surveillance from multiple agencies. Every move of his was being noted, every call screened. As the advisor to the DNLA, he was the link between the underground leadership and the government. For me, he had become the only bridge that made those earlier programs possible. But he was a tough man to convince. His thinking was straight: "Either my way or the highway."

He still hadn't forgiven me for refusing judima (the special local wine),[3] and he reminded me of it every now and then with a half-joking spark in his eyes. But beneath his hard exterior, there was something softer…a deep reverence for Gurudev. In every conversation, no matter how serious the topic, he would eventually say: "Please convey our *pranams* to Gurudev; ask for his blessings."

There was helplessness in his tone, but also a prayer. As if he carried the weight of his people on his shoulders and didn't know where else to place it. That mix of strength and vulnerability stayed with me.

---

[3] 'The Real Boot Camp' details more about this.

So we fixed a day. Nothing formal, nothing announced. Just a simple message: *We should meet Gurudev. The door is open.*

I could sense a change in Mukteshwar ji's tone. The tough, "my-way-or-the-highway" attitude was still there, but something inside him had softened. Maybe the pressure from the agencies was becoming too much. Maybe the inner conflict was finally catching up with him. Or maybe, like all of us, he just wanted a way out… a clean one.

When I told him Gurudev would meet us, he didn't argue. He didn't negotiate. He simply said, "Let me speak to the boys. We will come."

For someone like him, that was as good as a yes.

For the first time, he let the guard drop. He said softly, "IB has been behind me… I'm getting mentally exhausted with all these meetings. Our cadres are suffering in the jungles. There are threats everywhere. All of us are stressed."

I looked at him and said, "Then tell this directly to Gurudev."

There was a brief silence. Then he nodded. "Yes… Let's meet Gurudev."

He didn't argue, he didn't push back, he just agreed. That itself showed how much pressure he had been carrying. He asked for a little time to manage things on his side. Within the next two days, we froze a date to travel to Bengaluru. Our appointment with Gurudev was already confirmed through Karthik ji.

I booked the tickets. And unlike the earlier trip, there was no confusion, no double-mindedness, no tension. We were going with one intention: to seek Gurudev's blessings and bring clarity.

We were scheduled to meet him at 4:30 p.m. on 23 January.

When Gurudev arrived, he glanced at us, smiled gently, and said, "*Ārām se milte hain…*"

Then he moved on to meet the waiting devotees.

That one line…calm, casual, almost effortless…eased the entire weight in the room. It was as if he already knew everything and simply wanted us to settle, breathe and not rush the moment.

I was still trying to understand Gurudev's words when we left for the evening *satsang*. The hall, the music, the energy… everything settled the mind. And just as the *satsang* ended, my phone buzzed. It was Karthik ji.

"Gurudev will meet you around 9:30 p.m.," he said.

That one line sent a wave of focus through all of us.

Etika ji, Mukteshwarji, and his Commander-in-Chief Naiding immediately rushed with me to Radha Kunj. It felt as if every step carried years of weight…hopes, fears, uncertainties…all moving silently toward one room.

Gurudev arrived around 9:45 p.m. He met two or three people before us, smiling as he always does, unhurried, present, completely at ease.

Then it was our turn.

There was no one else in the room. Just us…and him.

The silence itself felt like a blessing. No rush, no formality, no barrier. For the first time, Mukteshwar ji and his commander-in-chief had space to speak openly; without fear, without pressure, without eyes watching every move.

They were free to express everything.

Gurudev greeted them with a warm *pranam*, and they immediately bowed and touched his lotus feet. No matter how many times I witness it, I'm always amazed by how naturally

Gurudev embraces people, how he makes them feel seen, valued, and completely at home. With him, everyone feels like family.

Gurudev going through the memorandum.

That evening, his presence was different. Softer. Deeper. He wasn't just a spiritual master; He felt like a mother, a guide, and a confidant all at once.

Mukteshwar ji began speaking first. Years of tension, fear and responsibility came out in his voice. He shared his worries openly: the pressure from the agencies, the condition of his cadres in the jungles, the heavy uncertainty around their future. Gurudev listened without interrupting, giving him the kind of attention that dissolves half the burden by itself.

Etika added a few more details, then the commander-in-chief spoke about the situation on the ground. I also briefed Gurudev on everything I had seen: their struggles, their living conditions, the constant threat they lived under.

At the heart of it, we all wanted the same thing: security, dignity, and a chance at a peaceful future for the entire DNLA team. We weren't asking for miracles. We were asking for direction... and a space where these young men could breathe again.

At one point, I said, "Gurudev... their team has learnt Sudarshan Kriya."

For a moment, Gurudev's face lit up. It was as if that one sentence opened a new doorway; a reminder that even in the toughest conditions, something pure had already touched their lives.

And I felt, silently, that the real turning point had finally arrived.

After we had shared everything, Mukteshwar ji handed over the memorandum to Gurudev. He received it with the same seriousness with which they had written it. And then something remarkable happened.

Gurudev began reading it line by line; not skimming, not rushing, but studying every point with complete attention. The room was silent, except for the soft sound of the pages being turned. It felt as if every word was being weighed, understood, and held with responsibility.

A very meaningful discussion unfolded that night.

With a mix of humility and firm clarity, Gurudev began summarizing their demands and concerns exactly as written in the memorandum. He mirrored their thoughts back to them so accurately that Mukteshwar ji and Etika exchanged looks of surprise. It was as if he had stepped directly into their world... their fears, their hopes, their expectations... and articulated it better than they could.

Their faces lit up. For the first time, I saw a sense of relief wash over them.

Then Gurudev went through each point again; this time, not just repeating, but guiding.

Gurudev looked at them and asked gently, "What is the strength of the Dima Hasao tribes?"

Mukteshwar ji replied, "Approximately 1.4 million."

Gurudev paused for a moment, then asked, "Do you think it is practical to demand a separate country... to run a nation landlocked inside India ... and expect to grow?"

A deep silence filled the room.

It was a question they had never really confronted. The idea of a separate nation had been carried for years, but no one had ever asked them about its practicality, its sustainability, its future. Mukteshwar ji didn't have an answer. He simply fell back into describing the suffering their people were going through. This time his voice was heavier, emotional.

Gurudev listened with full attention... not interrupting, not judging.

Then he asked another simple but piercing question: "Is there anyone among you who can actually lead such a nation... run it, guide it, hold it?"

That question struck them deeply. Again, they had no answer. Their eyes revealed more than their words... confusion, emotion, and the weight of years of struggle. You could feel their hearts speaking louder than their voices.

Gurudev softened his tone and said, "I understand the pain you go through. It is important, very important, to preserve your culture, your identity. The Dima Hasao heritage must not be lost. It must be protected for future generations."

Then he added, firmly but compassionately, "However, this should not come through violence. There are peaceful ways to achieve what you want."

He looked at them with deep affection and appreciation. "See, you have undergone years of hardship living in the jungles. Your commitment is admirable. But think of the next generation. So much more can be achieved if you use your soft potential...your intelligence, your culture, your leadership... for a better future, and for a better society."

In that moment, the air in the room changed.

It was the first time someone had acknowledged their sacrifices without glorifying their suffering, and shown them a dignified, peaceful path forward.

The room went completely still.

Mukteshwar ji lowered his eyes. Naiding, usually so firm and unreadable, was quietly staring at the floor. Etika's face had softened; his breath had changed. It was the kind of silence that doesn't come from fear; it comes from being understood after years of carrying a burden alone.

For the first time, someone had spoken to them not as rebels, not as suspects, not as a threat, but as human beings with a history, a culture, a wound, and a longing for dignity.

When Gurudev acknowledged their pain, something inside them melted.

When he asked those two simple questions...practical, direct, unavoidable...something inside them shifted.

Naiding, the commander-in-chief, who rarely spoke, finally raised his head. His voice was low, almost trembling: "Gurudev! We have never heard these things from anyone. People fear us, avoid us...no one sits with us like this."

Mukteshwar ji added softly, "We only wanted our people to survive, we didn't know how else to protect them."

Their words weren't polished. They didn't know how to express what was happening inside. But their eyes said everything: *respect, relief, confusion, hope, and a kind of surrender that doesn't come from defeat... but from being finally understood.*

In that moment, it was clear: The conversation wasn't just changing their minds. It was touching their hearts.

Gurudev offered his wisdom on every issue: what was practical, what was emotional, what needed patience, and what needed action.

He didn't promise shortcuts. He showed a path.

By the time he finished, it was clear that they had not merely been heard, they had been understood.

Even after listening to everything, Mukteshwar ji returned to his core demand. "Gurudev, we still want an independent country," he insisted.

He began again, recounting the struggles his people had faced. You could see how deeply the history lived in him; the memories were not political, they were personal.

Gurudev looked straight into his eyes and whispered gently, yet firmly, "Mukteshwar ji… These demands are not practical. You must be realistic."

"Getting a separate country *inside* our country… this is a redundant ask," Gurudev said softly.

But more than his words, it was his presence that changed the room.

The atmosphere felt calmer, clearer, as if the heaviness that had accompanied the idea of separation was suddenly being lifted by something higher.

Then Gurudev asked, "Why limit yourself only to Dima Hasao? Why not think of Assam… and of India?"

Gurudev shifted their perspective in one sentence.

"Instead of asking for a separate nation, you can strengthen your own nation. And you can do it through your culture, your community, and peaceful engagement."

Gurudev continued, "All your concerns, all your rights, all your aspirations… these can be achieved with mass participation of your people. Present your wishes unitedly. We will support your cause."

The words "we will support your cause" hit them deeply. It was dignity being returned to them.

Then Gurudev added one final line: "Violence never brings peace."

The room fell quiet again.

"But Gurudev... We don't trust the government," Mukteshwar ji said. "There is a trust deficiency. Why should we surrender when there is zero trust?"

His voice was firm, but underneath it, you could hear fear; not for himself, but for the people depending on him.

Gurudev replied calmly, "To come into the mainstream, you have to work with the government, isn't it?"

He paused, letting the words settle.

Then he added, "Why don't you place *realistic* demands before them?"

"You can become a political representative of your people," he continued.

"You can work for their upliftment. Skill-training can be provided so that your cadres have sustainable livelihoods. They can live with self-esteem."

Their faces softened as he spoke.

"You can even ask the government for land," Gurudev said. "Start farming. Build your economy. Then your people will not need to migrate or struggle for employment."

The conversation was going deeper than any of us expected. Every sentence was breaking an old belief, and offering a new possibility.

Etika, who had been quietly listening, finally said, "But we don't trust the government." His voice carried years of disappointment.

Mukteshwar ji was adamant, "The government promises… but delivers nothing. What if we surrender and nothing happens? Then all these years of tapas go to waste."

You could feel the insecurity behind his words… the fear that surrender would erase their sacrifices, their identity, their purpose.

Many people wait months just to get a glimpse of Gurudev, a single hello, a fleeting darshan. And here he was giving every minute, every attention, to the smallest detail of their lives, their fears, their future. Every moment felt like a "wow."

Then came the sentence that changed the energy of the room.

"We cannot surrender to the government," Mukteshwar ji said quietly, "but we can surrender to *you,* Gurudev."

He looked up with a mixture of vulnerability and trust.

"What if… what if *you* can be our interlocutor with the government?" he asked.

It wasn't a negotiation tactic.

It was a plea for trust… the kind that comes from the heart.

For the first time that night, the possibility of peace felt real.

Gurudev looked straight into their eyes, and without even a second of hesitation said,

"Yes, I am ready to be the interlocutor."

Then he turned to me and said, "Vishnu, you draft all our discussions and meet me at the earliest."

I simply nodded. That one instruction carried the responsibility of a future we had only hoped for. We took *prasad,* and Gurudev gently tapped Etika's cheeks… a small, affectionate gesture that melted the intensity of the moment. The room softened instantly. Laughter came in, lightness returned, and suddenly there was a joyful, almost childlike energy around us.

Gurudev asked them whether they were comfortable in the ashram. "This is your home," he added.

After submission of new memorandum.

To anyone else, these might sound like simple words. But to them... people who had spent years in fear, displacement, and uncertainty... it was healing. An assurance. A sense of belonging. A sense of safety they hadn't felt in a long time. This is what home-coming feels like.

In one meeting, He had given them something the jungles, the negotiations, and the conflict never could: HOPE.

And more than hope, He offered *himself*—to stand between them and the government.

All of us were stunned. None of us had expected this level of commitment from him. We were happy, relieved, and overwhelmed; but the clock was ticking. We had only a day left to reach a common conclusion and present something concrete.

The meeting lasted about thirty minutes, though it felt like an entire chapter of life compressed into a single moment.

Gurudev moved on to his online meetings afterward.

We stepped out quietly.

As we walked out of Radha Kunj, I began summarising everything, every point, every guidance, while walking alongside Mukteshwar ji. He listened with full attention, his face thoughtful, almost softened. The hard lines of worry that had shadowed him for years had eased.

For the first time, there was clarity in the air.

And I knew the next 24 hours were going to shape the future of an entire community.

Mukteshwar ji and Etika were overjoyed. The moment they stepped out of Radha Kunj, you could see it in their faces; a mix of relief, gratitude, and disbelief.

For them, it felt as though they had found their Krishna in the middle of their own Mahabharat. Someone who understood them, who guided them, and who was ready to stand by them.

I too was amazed. With everything Gurudev handles... millions of people, global projects, humanitarian work... he still took on this completely new responsibility without a second thought. It was a direct lesson for me in what true leadership means... how real responsibility is taken. Not with noise, but with quiet, decisive action.

When I reached home that night, sleep just wouldn't come. My mind kept replaying his words. I didn't want to miss a single instruction, a single point of clarity, a single nuance. The responsibility of compiling the entire summary, and presenting it to him the next evening, was weighing on me; not with pressure, but with purpose.

On the other hand, Etika was almost relaxed now. The load on his mind had reduced because the real work was on

Mukteshwar ji and me. We had to rewrite the entire charter; the "Demands 2.0," as we started calling it.

But this time, it wasn't just a list of demands. It was a vision, a beacon of hope, a *sankalpa,* an intention to create a violence-free society… and to reclaim dignity through peaceful means.

Every word mattered now.

We weren't drafting a negotiation paper. We were drafting a new beginning.

The next morning, I arranged a laptop in the SSPT office and got to work. I began drafting the full summary of our discussion from the night before. Mukteshwar ji sat beside me, editing it as I wrote.

But to my surprise, when he reviewed the document, he added his same old points again— a new country, expansion of Dima Hasao, all the earlier demands that Gurudev had already addressed with such clarity.

Looking at the document, it felt as if nothing from the night before had registered. The only new line he added was: "DNLA prays Gurudev Sri Sri Ravi Shankar ji to play the interlocutor with the Government of India, the Government of Assam, DPSC Civil/DNLA, Arms Organisation."

Everything else remained unchanged.

I reminded him of Gurudev's guidance.

I explained each point again.

He nodded every time, agreed every time, but would not change the demands.

And so the discussion restarted… From scratch.

It went on for six straight hours.

Six hours of explaining, re-explaining, reasoning, and grounding the conversation back to reality.

Six hours of him slipping into old thinking, then slowly coming back.

Six hours of phone interruptions, side discussions in the local language with his team, and long pauses where he simply stared at the screen, torn between the past and the future.

I won't lie; I was getting irritated, frustrated, and at times felt completely out of options.

But deep inside, one thing kept me steady: "Gurudev suggested this." That was my anchor.

Slowly, point by point, the eight demands started taking a new shape.

Sometimes he would argue. Sometimes he would silence his own doubts. Sometimes he looked emotional. And sometimes he would go quiet, speak to his team in their language, and finally nod.

By the end of six hours, we agreed.

It wasn't easy for him. It wasn't easy for me. But it was necessary.

Once we finished, I called Nakul Dhawan ji, our publications head, to review the final charter. He read through it carefully and added a few grammatical corrections and structural improvements.

At last, the document looked coherent, respectful, and aligned with the path Gurudev had shown.

It had taken all morning, all patience; but we finally had the Charter of Demands 2.0.

We were finally ready to print. Hours of back-and-forth arguments, clarifications, and careful rewriting had brought us to a clean, aligned Charter of Demands. Just then, Karthik ji called.

"Vishnu, Gurudev will meet you again at 9:30 p.m. in Radha Kunj."

It was perfect timing. We were prepared, the document was ready, and everything was falling into place.

But while I was still speaking to Karthik ji, something unexpected happened.

To my utter shock, Mukteshwar ji quietly typed out two more non-negotiable points at the end of the document... and immediately printed the letter.

My heart dropped.

I was furious, not because of the points themselves, but because the core instruction from Gurudev was being bent again.

Both of us had something at stake: His ideology was being challenged. And my Guru's instruction was being challenged.

The frustration hit so strongly that for a moment, I didn't know what to say. It felt like all the effort from the morning had been undone in a single moment.

Without thinking twice, I called Etika.

Before I could even start speaking, he said: "*Vishnu ji... hum log Gurudev ka hi baat mānenge. Aap chintā mat kijiye.*"

I let out a deep breath. A genuine sigh of relief.

He continued, "We don't want to dilute our weightage, that's why he added those points. But whatever Gurudev says... we will follow."

Hearing those words eased everything. The irritation. The frustration. The fear of betraying the clarity Gurudev had given.

It became clear once again: their heart was in the right place, but they just didn't know how to let go of decades of fear and old thinking all at once.

And then something shifted in me.

A neutral perspective... almost a witness consciousness... quietly dawned.

The irritation, the push, the frustration; all of it loosened. A kind of peace rose from within. I dropped everything at the feet of the Divine and simply allowed things to unfold.

We waited for Gurudev at Radha Kunj.

When he walked in, he greeted us with the same gentle smile as the night before. He looked genuinely pleased to see us. There was nothing hurried in his movements; his presence alone settled the air.

He took the final demand draft in his hands and began reading. Then he looked straight into my eyes.

In that single glance, he saw everything: the helplessness I felt earlier, the struggle of convincing them, the emotional tug-of-war between logic and loyalty, and the quiet surrender that had risen inside me.

He knew exactly what had been happening in everyone's mind…theirs, and mine.

That moment said more than words could.

Gurudev gently placed the document on the table and said, "I am keeping this letter. You can send a copy to the Chief Minister, the Governor, and the Home Ministry. There will be tough times…but I am with you. I will be your interlocutor."

Those words settled everything.

Then he turned to me again and said with quiet firmness, "Ensure their tickets are taken care of."

I replied immediately, "Gurudev, it's already taken care of."

He nodded softly, as though acknowledging not just the answer, but the intention behind it.

Gurudev blessed all of us.

Etika, overwhelmed, bowed again and held Gurudev's feet. "*Gurudev… hum aapke sharan mein aaye hain.*"

Gurudev smiled, pulled his cheeks gently, and reassured him, "I am with you." There was something timeless in that moment; a reassurance that did not come from authority, but from pure compassion.

A new chapter had just opened...quietly, beautifully, divinely.

The meeting ended, and Gurudev moved on to meet others.

We stepped aside, but our eyes remained fixed on him. None of us spoke for a moment. We were simply absorbing what had just happened.

You could see the shift in them instantly...the joy, the confidence, the relief.

They congratulated each other like soldiers who had finally found a commander they could trust with their lives. Just a few words from the Master, and the entire energy of the group had lifted. All the tiredness, the arguments, the heaviness of the past twenty-four hours had disappeared.

As Gurudev began to leave the hall, they spontaneously shouted, "Jai Gurudev!"

Gurudev acknowledged them with a gentle blink of his eyes—small, subtle, but powerful enough to make them feel personally seen.

A small chase began behind him, just like devotees do. And truly, something had changed.

They were no longer negotiating leaders. They were no longer guarded, defensive, doubtful.

On the way back, I turned to Mukteshwar ji and said, "I'm sorry for having been harsh today."

He laughed and held my shoulder, *"Gurudev hamara kam kar denge. Aur aapko hum chhodenge nahi... chahe aap kitne bhi rust ho jao."*

We both burst out laughing. All the tension of the day dissolved.

Two meetings with Gurudev within twenty-four hours; and that one assurance, "I am with you," felt like the Divine whispering that the storm would pass soon.

Whatever heaviness they had carried for years—fear, uncertainty, doubt—it had begun to dissolve. The return journey was simple. No noise, no tension. Just a quiet, steady trust in their hearts.

I still didn't know when their official surrender would come, but somewhere, silently, I had witnessed something more important: they had already surrendered to the Master. Their resistance, their ideology, their guardedness… it had all softened.

The next morning, we met Bhanumaa. She was exactly what they needed after those intense two days: an epitome of divinity, calmness and motherly grace. She welcomed them with sweets and listened patiently as they narrated the story of Maata Hidamba with childlike excitement.

We all sat at her lotus feet, and the atmosphere shifted immediately. There was a softness in the room, a presence that made the mind fall silent on its own.

I told her, "Gurudev has offered to be their interlocutor."

She smiled gently and said, "The Divine will fulfill all your wishes."

Those words had warmth, reassurance, and the strength of someone who sees beyond situations. We felt truly blessed, as though the universe itself was giving us a nod of confirmation.

After we stepped out, Etika came to me with tears shining in his eyes and said, "In Bhanumaa… I got a glimpse of Devi Divine."

I replied, "She *is* our Devi Divine."

He had sensed something rare, something devotees spend years waiting to feel: the unfathomable grace, the stillness, the depth. Sitting at her lotus feet, all the mental gymnastics, all the tension, all the leftover anxiety simply disappeared. We were completely rested, as if our minds had been switched off and rebooted into peace.

Later that evening, I drove them to the airport. As we stood near the entrance, Etika suddenly hugged me tightly. With full emotion, he whispered, *"Gurudev... Bhagwan hain."*

He could no longer hide his feelings. Everything he had been holding inside for years...fear, hope, surrender...came out in that one sentence.

I smiled and said softly, "We'll catch up soon."

And as they walked toward the terminal, I knew deeply that something irreversible had happened inside them.

A transformation had begun; not through ideology or negotiation, but through grace.

For the first time in my life, I understood what surrender truly means.

Before this journey, I thought I was guiding others. But in truth, I was the one being transformed.

12

Fluoride Nilogon

Solving the fluoride menace through seva and miracles…

Our Kamal ji—a true yogi and a devoted soul–comes from Techalangjun. One day, he began suffering from severe back pain. I was surprised and concerned, wondering what could have caused this sudden discomfort.

When I asked him, Kamal ji simply said, "The water in our village is not good; that is why I am not feeling well." At first, I could not relate his back pain to the water quality in his village.

However, upon further enquiry, I discovered a disturbing reality. The groundwater in his village is naturally contaminated with fluoride levels (3.1mg/litre) which is far above the safe limit (<1.5mg/litre) for human consumption. As a result, almost every child in the village suffers from bone deformities and skeletal issues.

It revealed a silent yet severe crisis—one that is invisible on the surface but deeply affects lives every day. A truly unique and alarming problem statement that calls for urgent attention.

The Art of Living foundation's connection with society is expressed through creative and compassionate projects that bring tangible and lasting change to people's lives. One such meaningful collaboration emerged with Tezpur University, where Dr. Robin Dutta ji designed a low-cost water filter capable of removing excess fluoride from drinking water.

Recognising the urgency of the situation in Techalangjun, Longbir ji submitted a proposal to the Karbi Anglong Autonomous Council. One fine evening, he came to me brimming with joy and enthusiasm. He said, "Vishnu ji, we have cracked a very beautiful project. The government has agreed to make The Art of Living the implementation agency to install these scientific filters designed by Tezpur University in the households of the Techalangjun area."

The news brought immense happiness. Kamal ji, in particular, was extremely excited. For him and his village, it was not just a project; it was hope, healing, and a promise of a healthier future.

My joy matched their enthusiasm. Longbirji told me, "We have to install these in 1,500 households, the direct beneficiaries of the project, besides at 10 community centers in the first phase."

A real transformation. Families would finally be able to drink clean water, free from the excessive fluoride that has been damaging bones, the nervous system, and even the teeth for generations.

But it wasn't simple. Many villagers had preconceived notions. They needed someone to guide them, to explain, to help them trust the filters and actually use them.

What we did have was solid; a foolproof design by Dr. Robin Dutta ji, a budget approved by the council, committed beneficiaries, and above all, the dedication and the will to make this happen.

Karthik ji, Gurudev's secretary, called me in the evening and asked if I could host a few international volunteers who wanted to do service in the Northeast for six to eight weeks.

I immediately said, "Yes. We have a project coming up and they can really help us."

Karthik ji checked with Gurudev, and we received approval to go ahead with the "Fluoride Nilogon" project. And to my surprise, their tickets were booked by the afternoon.

A new team was on its way, sincere seekers from another part of the world.

A wonderful group of four: Raul Alvarez from Asunción, Paraguay; Sergio de la Mano from La Plata, Argentina; Ana Carolina Gomez from Quilmes, Argentina; and Mateo from Venado Tuerto, Argentina. They had been serving at the Bengaluru Ashram, and this time, they were travelling to the Northeast.

The fantastic Four group welcomed traditionally at Diphu Ashram.

I had hosted international volunteers before; Dr. Barbara Ferrando from Italy, Ariex Bax, Pamela, and others; so I had a fair sense of what made them feel comfortable and what could be challenging for them.

Still, with our limited resources at the ashram, we made space for them. They were to arrive the next day.

I checked with Longbir ji and said, "Alright, let's now discuss the project, what exactly needs to be executed."

He replied calmly, "We just have to install the filters. That's all."

I felt reassured. But when I went through the technical documents of the filters, the reality unfolded. The setup was far more complex than it sounded. We needed limestone, phosphoric acid, specially designed buckets, measuring cans, proper installation spaces, a verified beneficiary list, nozzles, taps; all in large quantities for 1,500 households! On top of that, we needed instructions translated into the local language and many other details.

I asked Longbir ji, "So where are all these materials?"

He replied, "We have to buy them."

"And where is the money?" I asked.

"The council will give," he said.

I was taken aback. We had spoken so strongly and confidently about this project, encouraging people to move forward, yet at this moment, we had no clear execution plan and no resources in hand.

Longbir ji also realized the gravity of the situation, and our guests were due to arrive later that evening. With no funds in hand and a complex project to execute, we decided to approach the PHE Department (Public Health Engineering Department) to understand the financial process.

We went early in the morning, knowing the office would start late. Time was ticking, and I had no idea what to tell our guests, who were arriving full of excitement and ready to work.

Around 11 a.m., we finally met the PHE engineer. He listened patiently and then said, "We will release the funds once the project is completed."

I explained our situation, how could we complete the work without any money to begin with? He insisted that this was how the rules worked and assured us that the bills would be cleared within six months.

I was extremely shocked. The missing link of the project was finances and resources, everything else was already in place. We discussed the matter with the officer, weighing every possible pro and con, but he was firm. The rules laid down by the government could not be changed or altered.

The Art of Living was the executing agency, but we would first have to invest around ₹20 lakhs and then wait six months for reimbursement. I realized this would again mean running from office to office, moving files for payments.

We had a choice: to decline the offer and live peacefully. But Kamal ji's smile, with his red-stained teeth and constant back pain, stayed with me. Along with that, the blessings of Gurudev, and the arrival of four *sevaks* who were on their way kept telling my heart to find a solution.

I used every bit of logic to convince the authorities to sanction funds for the project. They, in turn, used every bit of logic to explain why they could not. We reached a deadlock, and it was already 2 p.m.

The officer then took us for lunch and suggested that we try meeting the honorable minister of PHED to see if he could help us move forward.

We rushed to meet Pradip Rongpi, the executive member of the Karbi Anglong Autonomous Council. He was a devotee of Gurudev and had met him several times. He listened to us patiently and then instructed the officer, *"Ensure the work does not suffer at any cost."*

We returned to the PHE office. After some time, the officer called me aside, handed me ₹2 lakhs, and said, *"Gurudev ka kaam nahi rukna chahiye"* (Gurudev's work should not stop).

He added that this was the first time he was giving money purely on hope and reverence, and told me to feel free to reach out to him if we needed any help.

We finally had seed money to kick-start the project.

The hand of the Divine was clearly visible. My prayers were answered. Longbirji and I rushed to pick up the Fantastic Four team!

Ana, Sergio, Mateo and Raul were welcomed with red Karbi poho and delicious meals. They were genuinely happy to be with us, and from the very first moment, we shared a warm and easy bond. Their focus was crystal clear, they had come to execute the 'Fluoride Nilogon Project', following the instructions of the Master.

Longbir ji looked at me and burst into laughter, the kind that comes once in a lifetime. He said, "What magic Gurudev does!"

People usually give money to officers to move files, and here the opposite had happened; the officers had given us money to execute the project.

By default, I became the program manager of the project.

The Fantastic Four were full of enthusiasm. Every now and then, they would ask me: "Vishnuji, when do we go? What do we do? Which filter? Where do we install it?" Question after question.

I smiled and said, "Rest well today. We'll discuss everything tomorrow."

Sergio again asked, with all his innocence, "So what would the filters look like and what impact will they make?"

I said, "We are waiting for some clearance, and we need 24 hours for the same."

The team, meanwhile, went to the nearby village and came back dressed in Karbi attire. They had gone to many houses, and people welcomed them with open hearts. Suddenly, news broke that four internationals had arrived at the Art of Living, and many people came to see them, take pictures, and enquire about their country. They too enquired about Karbi and were quick in learning local words, traditions, greetings, and simple ways to communicate. Everything was running on autopilot, and I was busy arranging and negotiating for filter items for a large-scale project covering 1,500 families.

I connected with our teacher, Pratap Das ji from Hojai, Assam, an Income Tax officer. He took me to a shop. I shared the full list of required items, and he agreed to supply everything within 48 hours, with payment to be made upfront.

I immediately broke my personal fixed deposits. As planned, the materials were to be shipped from Kolkata to Guwahati, and then onward to Dokmoka in Karbi Anglong.

Meanwhile, Longbir ji made arrangements to use a school premise in Techalangjun, where we could set up our base camp. Our local teachers Aarti, Bina and Reena, along with our volunteers Anjana and Bir, were already there, ready to support the work.

We packed all the essentials—cylinders, stoves, utensils and groceries—and began the transition to our base camp. We booked a small guesthouse to stay in and set up a temporary kitchen.

As the project began, challenges came up every single day. Yet, grace walked alongside us, helping us overcome each one. The locals pitched in wholeheartedly, and there was something magical about seeing international volunteers executing the project hand-in-hand with the local community.

Each day followed a rhythm. We would wake up early, do *sadhana,* and then begin the work; sanitizing the villages, preparing beneficiary lists, cooking food, etc. People would arrive to collect buckets, taps, limestone and materials. We would then go from house to house to install the filters, providing phosphoric acid supplies, and patiently educate the families on how to use the system and drink the water after 24 hours.

In every home, we were received with deep reverence.

And in every installation, it felt like something magical was unfolding.

Post the installation of Fluoride Nilogon filters.

Gradually, we began setting up community filters as well. We were so deeply absorbed in the work that by evening, I would be completely exhausted, often without the energy to even eat. Kamal ji and Bina ji, despite being physically drained themselves, would lovingly cook and serve food to all of us.

Gurudev Sri Sri Ravi Shankar
@Gurudev

Due to high fluoride content, the water in Karbi Anglong, Assam causes red teeth & bone-related problems in the locals there. Our Prof. Robin Dutta has made a fluoride removing filter. This @ArtofLiving project will provide drinking water to 6500+ homes & 50 public campuses.

Horen Sing Bey and 2 others

3:53 PM · Sep 27, 2019

Gurudev's tweet about Fluordie Nilogon.

Our spirits, however, remained high. Day by day, we started reaching deeper into the interiors, places with almost no access. People carried the filters on their backs or on bicycles. We would walk several miles to inspect the sites, set up the systems, and then return to ensure everything was working properly.

More and more people began joining us. Children who once hid their smiles because their teeth were damaged by fluoride began smiling openly again, filled with confidence.

We were happy, constantly busy, and every filter installed felt like a light of hope, an affirmation that humanity still exists, and that a higher power was guiding and taking care of us.

As Gurudev says, "Seva means doing something for someone else without expectations."

As we were nearing the completion of the project, a thought arose, of inviting the governor of Assam to inaugurate it. Without a second thought, Honourable Jagdish Mukhi ji, the then governor of Assam, graciously gave his consent to inaugurate the project.

Inviting the governor to dedicate the project.

The news spread like wildfire. With his excellency's visit confirmed, the administration came forward in full support.

What followed felt almost unbelievable. Within 12 hours, the roads leading to our base camp were completed. Roads that had remained untouched for 75 years were suddenly completed overnight, without approvals or long procedures. It was beyond imagination.

A ground was prepared, a stage was set up, and all the beneficiaries were invited. Our team stretched themselves beyond their limits, working day and night to ensure everything was ready. Every detail was coordinated closely with the Governor's Office to warmly welcome him.

It was also perfectly timed, as our international volunteers were scheduled to leave for Bengaluru the very next day after the event.

On 4 December 2019, the CAA (Citizenship Amendment Act) protests broke out in Assam and spread like wildfire. The passage of the Act triggered massive protests across India. In Assam and other northeastern states, people opposed the grant of Indian citizenship to refugees or immigrants, regardless of religion, fearing it would alter the region's demographic balance.

Soon, the protests reached Karbi Anglong. Late in the evening, just a day before the event, I received a call from the governor's secretariat informing us that the inauguration had to be called off, as it was too risky for the governor to travel.

Sensing the seriousness of the situation, I accepted the decision. Our work was almost complete. And yet, by Gurudev's grace, the roads to the region had already been built overnight, something far beyond our comprehension!

The protests escalated rapidly and caused heavy damage to public property. A few lives were lost in the riots. Tires were burned on the roads, and fear spread everywhere, especially along the national highway. It was a terrifying experience.

Naturally, it deeply scared our international volunteers. They contacted the Bengaluru secretariat to inform them about the situation. We were safe inside the base camp, but the circumstances outside were extremely challenging. When internationals are involved, even a small incident can quickly become an international issue.

Karthik ji called me several times. The responsibility for their safety was entirely on me. While we were safe for the moment, there was no way to predict the next trigger for violence.

I reported the situation to the Doboka police station, and the officer-in-charge strongly advised that, given the gravity of the unrest, the foreign volunteers should leave Assam as soon as possible.

We decided to begin our journey at midnight, so they could catch their scheduled early-morning flight from Guwahati to Bengaluru.

That night, another realization struck me: I had no cash in hand. The funds were in the bank, but we barely had any physical cash. I had earlier requested Longbir ji to arrange cash for the governor's inauguration event, but with the CAA protests unfolding, everything had come to a standstill.

A new problem stared us in the face. We had no money to fuel the car to Guwahati. There was absolutely no scope for reinforcement, and time was critical; the international volunteers *had* to catch their flight.

So I told the team, *"Today, we will earn guru dakshina."*

From morning till evening, we went door to door, visiting every household. We checked on their well-being and humbly asked for *guru dakshina*. The villagers were deeply grateful. Some offered a pumpkin, some chilies or tomatoes, a little paddy. A few gave ₹10, ₹20 and the like ... whatever they could.

We continued house to house, collecting Guru Dakshina with humility and gratitude. By the end of the day, I was holding a bundle of coins and cash gathered by our entire team; a collective offering that would carry us forward.

As planned, we had local police escorting us up to the national highway. The moment we reached it, the scene was terrifying: burning tires everywhere, flames lighting up the darkness, fear hanging thick in the air.

After travelling about 50 kilometers towards Guwahati, our driver turned to me and said quietly, "We have fuel for only about 20 minutes."

The roads were deserted. We stopped at the first petrol pump. Closed. The second, closed. Third, fourth, fifth, sixth ... all were shut.

By now, the vehicle was gasping for fuel. I kept praying to Gurudev; we were stranded in the middle of the road, and somehow, we *had* to reach the airport.

We reached the seventh petrol pump. It too was closed.

It was 2:30 a.m.

Suddenly, a stranger appeared out of nowhere and started talking to me. He asked, "You want petrol, right?"

I said, "Yes."

"Come," he said, and he began filling our tank.

As he refueled the car, I couldn't help but notice that he was a pious Muslim. I asked him how he happened to be there at that hour. He replied, "A baba with a white beard woke me up in my dream and told me to come and fuel this car."

In that moment, I knew, my prayers were not just heard. They were already in motion.

We filled the car and rushed to Guwahati Airport, reaching safely around 4 a.m. I thanked the international team, and they were deeply grateful as well. In my heart, I felt a quiet guilt; I was seeing them off without a proper farewell. They had no money either, and in our eyes, we could feel the unspoken emotion.

It was a simple, heartfelt goodbye.

As I turned to walk away, Sergio tapped me on the back and handed me an envelope. He said, "Vishnu ji, I forgot to give you my *guru dakshina*. Here it is."

I was stunned. When I opened the envelope, it had around ₹2,210. I took ₹10, returned the envelope to him, and said with a smile, "Have nice dosas at the airport."

He laughed, took it back, and replied, "No, we'll have idlis." We burst into laughter.

They left, full of excitement, and I was filled with immense gratitude. The project had been completed, a true roller-coaster journey.

When we later reviewed the budget, we realized we had gone beyond our original targets. Instead of 1,500 filters, we reached 1,630 families and set up 15 community centers in Phase 1 itself! Beyond that, the government sanctioned a new pipeline, giving villagers a dedicated water connection.

Gurudev also tweeted about the Fluoride Nilogon Project, a reminder that wherever there is humanity, there is divinity quietly supporting it.

Later, we built steps leading to our main meditation hall using the *guru dakshina* offered by the villagers. My thought process was simple: those who had contributed, in whatever way they could, would symbolically enter the Vaikuntha Hall of our Diphu Ashram through the merit of their offerings and be part of our prayers.

In time, the work order was processed, and we returned the money to the PHED officer. He accepted it with folded hands, visibly moved, amazed that he too had become part of one of the first service projects to be executed with such dedication, commitment and joy.

Love in action is *seva,* and spirituality is that which uplifts the spirit. Through Gurudev's wisdom and grace, this service reached people who now have access to pure drinking water.

We also paid a royalty fee to Tezpur University at the rate of ₹1 per filter, which they accepted as a token of gratitude.

Even now, whenever Kamal ji visits the villages, our volunteers continue to educate families and update them on the correct usage and maintenance of the filters.

Gurudev's picture on each filter carries a quiet message... that a saint is blessing them and watching over them through all odds of life. We remain deeply grateful and blessed to have been instruments in this journey.

13

The Landslide and the Unwavering Smile

The roads vanished... yet we were being led.

One of the state's cabinet ministers, Nandita Gorlosa ji, from the spiritually rich land of Dima Hasao in Assam, was divinely guided to receive the blessed darshan of Gurudev during the *Chintan Shibir* at Kaziranga. For a long time, her heart had been silently calling out to the Master. After doing the Sahaj Samadhi program with me, a deeper stillness and longing arose within her, as though her soul had already surrendered at his lotus feet, waiting only for that sacred moment of Gurudev's physical presence and blessing.

In the mysterious play of *guru tattva,* it is no mere coincidence that her birthday falls on 13 May, the same auspicious day on which the Master himself incarnated to awaken humanity. Even more wondrous is the fact that the chief executive member of Dima Hasao, Shri Debolal Gorlosa ji, also shares this blessed birth date. It feels as though the land of Dima Hasao is vibrating with a hidden divine geometry, silently proclaiming its deep connection with the Master's consciousness.

Haflong, the district capital, often revered as the *Mini Switzerland of the North East,* appears as a manifestation of divine artistry. Its rolling green hills, mist-covered valleys, and untouched landscapes feel like a living meditation crafted by the elements themselves. In its silence, one can hear the whisper of ancient wisdom; in its beauty, one can feel the presence of the Divine Mother; and in its stillness, the subtle grace of Gurudev flows like an invisible river. Every path, every cloud, every breeze seems to chant the Divine's name, embedding eternal memories in the heart of every seeker who steps upon this sacred ground.

Despite her extremely demanding schedule, Nandita ji and her family had lovingly planned to meet Gurudev. Our appointment had been scheduled, flight tickets were confirmed, and we were meant to fly to Bengaluru the very next day. Everything seemed to be moving toward that divine moment. However, that very day, nature took a sudden and unprecedented turn. A massive landslide struck the Dima Hasao district, an impact so severe that the elders said nothing like it had been witnessed in the last 50 years! Though floods and landslides are not uncommon in the region, the devastation this time was unparalleled.

In that moment, duty became worship. With an indescribably heavy heart, we chose to surrender our personal longing at the feet of Gurudev and answer the call of service first, deciding to meet him at a later time. It felt as though the Divine itself was testing our surrender and strength.

The rain poured relentlessly from the heavens, as if the skies too were in turbulence. Haflong became completely cut off by both rail and road. Several railway bridges had collapsed, and the land that once echoed with serenity was immersed in uncertainty. There was little that could be done externally. All that remained was to wait, surrender, and pray, trusting that Gurudev's invisible hand was protecting the people and holding the land in His grace.

I was at our Diphu Ashram when the news reached me, and an intense urge arose within to stand with our people in Dima Hasao in whatever way possible. I immediately connected with Etika, but the response was heartbreaking; the roads were completely blocked. Landslides had always been a part of life in these hills, yet this time, the scale of destruction had crossed all known limits.

Having been part of several flood relief initiatives across Assam in the past, I could deeply feel the silent suffering and uncertainty that the people must have been going through. And yet, even in such moments of despair, one truth stood out clearly: our people are not greedy. With even a little help, they make space for others. That selflessness, that innate spirit of sharing, is the true essence of human values.

It is the revival of these values that holds the key to a stress-free, violence-free society — a world rooted in compassion and unity. This, in its deepest sense, is the very mission of Gurudev.

Moved by this spirit of service, we quickly formed a small response team. Drawing on our previous experiences, we gathered essential supplies—groceries, rice, matchsticks, medicines—preparing ourselves to reach out in whatever way possible. But our greatest challenge was access. With the roads destroyed and landslides continuing, all external efforts felt helpless. I could do nothing but wait, pray, and remain alert, ready to serve the moment the path opened.

In the midst of this uncertainty, Longbir ji arranged a trolley truck, and I packed it to its fullest capacity so that, when the opportunity came, not a single moment would be wasted in serving the needy. Yet, sitting there and watching from a distance as people suffered was one of the most painful experiences of all, a silent prayer rising from the heart for their safety, protection, and strength under Gurudev's unseen grace.

One fine day, I just prayed to Gurudev and started towards Dima Hasao. My driver was very confident and experienced, and as soon as we hit the national highway, we encountered a roadblock. It was drizzling too and we were stuck there for few hours. We had a choice to go back, but we continued.

As we approached Maibong, we had been slowly racing with nature's hide and seek. The situation was very miserable and with prayers in our hearts, we reached the Maibong rescue center where people had assembled for safety, on account of the landslides. With folded hands and teary eyes, we distributed all the essential items we had brought. Many of the locals held my hands and said, *"God has sent you."* When they saw Gurudev's photograph, they bowed down in deep reverence. Some shared that they had gone to sleep peacefully the night before, and when they woke up, *everything was gone:* their homes, their belongings, except the clothes on their bodies. And yet, what moved me the most was the unwavering smile, the quiet dignity, and the complete acceptance of the present moment etched on every face.

In that silence, a profound lesson dawned upon me: how deeply one can remain joyful and peaceful with the bare minimum. It was living wisdom, not spoken but embodied.

By the time we began our return, the government machinery had already started taking charge of the situation. We felt truly blessed to have been among the first responders to offer trauma relief, and deeply grateful that Gurudev had used us as instruments. Though the rain had finally subsided, hope was rising everywhere. There was so much to be done and so few resources, yet we felt held by the unfathomable grace of the Master. Slowly, support began to pour in from different directions, and long-term plans for flood and landslide relief started to take shape under his divine guidance.

That journey into Dima Hasao was not just a relief mission; it became a living *sadhana*. Every fallen tree, every broken road, every trembling hillside felt like a reminder of the impermanence of this world. And yet, in the midst of destruction, I witnessed something eternal, the indomitable spirit of humanity. I realized that when one serves in the awareness of the Master, *seva* becomes prayer, and action becomes meditation.

As we moved through the damaged land, I could feel an invisible protection surrounding us. There were moments when the path ahead looked completely impossible; yet somehow, every time, a way opened up. A fallen rock here, a narrow passage there, a sudden clearing in the fog, it was as though Gurudev himself was guiding our vehicle, watching over each turn of the wheel. In the middle of chaos, there was an unexplainable calm within me, a deep knowing that *nothing could harm us in his presence.*

From that day onward, my relationship with Gurudev transformed. It was no longer limited to longing for his physical presence. I began to feel him in the wind, in the rain, in the suffering of people, and in the courage that rose to serve them. That devastating phase became a sacred initiation; a moment where the disciple in me dissolved a little more, and the devotee in me surrendered completely.

Dima Hasao no longer remained just a place on the map. For me, it became a living temple of faith, a reminder that even in destruction, the Master is building something far greater within us.

In that silence within,
I have experienced a Presence that is unfathomable
Entered a space that is Infinite;
Merged with a time that is Eternal;
And in that stillness... I have experienced Myself.

Gurudev,
With you, I have learnt a new expression—smile.
With you, my heart has been filled, not with emotions, but with pure love.
With you, I have discovered a connection beyond words —
In devotion, in surrender; I'm now home.

From you,
I have received blessings...
Krupa, flowing like an endless river through my being.

Aho!
I have experienced you—
As infinite love, as eternal devotion,
As unfathomable grace,
As a smile in every moment.

And finally,
I have realized...
The Guru I was searching for outside
Has always lived within me.

We continued with numerous service projects, and one deeply impactful initiative was the distribution of solar lights in West

Karbi Anglong. Moved by the silent suffering of the people living along the remote borders of Karbi Anglong and Meghalaya, Gurudev, in his compassion, even spoke about this through his words, drawing attention to their hidden pain.

In those regions, there were no proper roads, no electricity, and life would dissolve into complete darkness after sunset. When the solar lights finally reached the villagers, it was as if a small sun had descended into their homes. Those simple lights became a beacon of hope, restoring not only visibility but also dignity, safety, and a renewed sense of belonging to the world.

In the eyes of the people, I did not see just gratitude; I saw faith rekindled. In that darkness, Gurudev's light had arrived in the form of *seva,* and I felt once again that it was not us who were serving, but Gurudev himself, working through us.

14

Tenzing Terang

Peace found a way in where guns once spoke.

With Gurudev's grace, Longki ji played an instrumental role in reaching out to militant organizations in Karbi Anglong, inspiring them to walk the path of non-violence: a path he himself had learned, experienced, and lived under Gurudev's guidance.

One by one, we engaged with these groups, and it became evident that they too were yearning for peace and a dignified accord with the government. Having Gurudev as their guiding light, and witnessing the courageous leadership of Longki ji, who had himself taken the bold step of joining the mainstream, deeply inspired them.

Inspired by the surrender of the UPLA, six militant organizations followed suit, surrendering to the Government of India and signing a historic peace accord in 2021. This marked a decisive shift from armed conflict to dialogue and democratic participation in Karbi Anglong. It is astonishing how a single light lit by Gurudev spread like fire, dissolving fear and conflict, and igniting a lasting transformation rooted in peace and harmony.

Following the accord, an umbrella organization was formed, uniting former cadres from multiple groups—including KLNLF, UPLA, KPLT-R, KPLT-C, KPLT-M and PDCK—with a shared mission to sustain peace and work towards rural economic upliftment and social development in the region.

The organizations that laid down arms include:

- Karbi Longri NC Hills Liberation Front (KLNLF)
- United People's Liberation Army (UPLA)
- People's Democratic Council of Karbi Longri (PDCK)
- Karbi People's Liberation Tigers (KPLT) — Run Rongpi faction
- KPLT — Ceasefire faction
- KPLT — Mensing Kramsa faction

On 4 September 2021, they signed a significant peace accord (Memorandum of Settlement) with the Government of India and the Government of Assam, bringing an end to decades of conflict in the Karbi Anglong region. Subsequently, a new collective platform—the Karbi Ex-Revolutionary United Forum (KERUF)—was formed. KERUF represents former armed groups from Karbi Anglong, Assam, and serves as a unified voice to ensure the effective implementation of the peace accord. Its mission includes rehabilitation of former cadres, promotion of development initiatives such as agriculture-based livelihoods, welfare programs, and sustained efforts toward economic upliftment and long-term peace in the region.

In a powerful symbolic moment, around 2,000 former militants, along with their leaders, travelled to New Delhi, affirming their commitment to a peaceful and prosperous society. This moment marked history in the making…an extraordinary transformation that stands as a testament to Gurudev's unfathomable grace and the silent yet profound magic of peace in action.

However, within a few months, the unforeseen impact of COVID-19 struck hard. Government rehabilitation schemes and initiatives aimed at integrating the former cadres into the mainstream came to a sudden halt. What had begun with hope and momentum was stalled by circumstances beyond anyone's control.

Around 2,000 former militants, who had already laid down their arms and stepped away from their past lives, were left struggling for basic livelihood. The situation became deeply distressing. Earlier, even while living in the jungles, they had found ways to survive and support their families. Now, having chosen peace and surrendered their weapons, they were confined, vulnerable, and almost entirely dependent on government welfare schemes—schemes that were functional, but moving at a "*lahe-lahe*" (very slow) pace.

As the hardships continued, many of the surrendered militants began expressing deep frustration, even directing their anger toward the leadership, as sustaining their families became increasingly difficult. After the surrender process, the organizational discipline that once bound them together gradually weakened, with cadres scattered across different locations and struggling in isolation.

In this state of uncertainty and despair, some former militants began entertaining extreme thoughts of forming a new militant organization, a new faction altogether. Such a step would have undone years of sincere efforts, trust-building, and peace-making. It threatened to reverse the hard-earned progress; all the good work and sacrifices made in the journey toward peace could go to waste.

This was a critical juncture, where the path of non-violence required renewed strength, guidance and timely intervention to prevent a return to conflict.

At this crucial moment, Longki ji met Gurudev's secretary, Krishna Sastry ji, who had come to our Diphu Ashram for a

Sanyam One Retreat. Longki ji shared his concerns openly; his emotional restlessness and growing insecurity were evident.

Krishna Sastry ji listened with great patience and compassion. After understanding the gravity of the situation, he suggested that the KERUF leadership come to Bengaluru and present their concerns directly to Gurudev.

Longki ji immediately reached out to the top leadership of **KERUF**, and without a second thought, they agreed to travel to Bengaluru and share their concerns with Gurudev. The situation on the ground was extremely fragile; at any moment, individual cadres could break away to form new factions.

I was deeply relieved and grateful to personally escort them to Bengaluru, hoping that this meeting would bring clarity, reassurance and renewed direction at a time when the peace process was hanging in a delicate balance.

Around eleven senior leaders from six militant organizations arrived in Bengaluru, and we immediately began a Happiness Program for them. I had the privilege of co-teaching the program with Juanfe, our art of living teacher from Colombia.

Among the participants was Pradip Terang, a founding figure of the insurgency in Karbi Anglong and the President of KERUF, along with his core team. For many of them, this was their first direct experience of Sudarshan Kriya. The impact was profound... powerful, uplifting, and deeply transformative.

In a single stroke, years of accumulated stress, fear, and tension seemed to dissolve. They felt an immediate sense of relief, inner calm, and belonging... as if they had finally come home. Though they were already familiar with Gurudev from afar, this experience prepared them inwardly for a personal, one-on-one interaction with the Master, with open hearts and settled minds.

The shift in their energy was unmistakable, signaling the beginning of yet another quiet but powerful transformation.

As per our appointment, we waited for Gurudev at Buddha Hall in the Vishalakshi Mantap. The moment Gurudev arrived, all of them bowed down in deep reverence and said with folded hands, "Gurudev, you brought us into the mainstream, but now we are facing a new problem."

Gurudev welcomed them warmly, draping shawls over their shoulders, and gently invited them to share their concerns in detail. One by one, they spoke of their challenges: the stalled rehabilitation, the pressure of sustaining their families, and the growing unrest among the cadres. Some expressed their desperation so strongly that they admitted, "We may be forced to form a new organization; we see no other option."

Gurudev listened with complete seriousness and unwavering attention. With immense compassion, he assured them of his love and full support, and firmly instructed them not to think along those lines. They had already tasted the peace of a non-violent life, yet their helplessness and anxiety were clearly visible.

Gurudev meeting former militants at Bengaluru Ashram.

In that moment, they were not hardened former militants; they were like children opening their hearts before their mother, seeking reassurance, protection and guidance. Gurudev held the space with silence, strength and grace, allowing their fears to dissolve in his presence.

After about fifteen minutes of interaction, Gurudev turned to me and asked me to prepare a detailed list of the cadres and arrange for bringing them to SSRDP for skill-development training. He also instructed me to meet Dr. Ashish Bhutani, who was then heading the Agriculture Department of the Government of Assam, to explore long-term livelihood solutions.

At the same time, Gurudev firmly reiterated that the cadres should be brought to Bengaluru for training, making his instruction unequivocal. There was no ambiguity in his direction; action had to begin immediately.

With this assurance and clarity, everyone returned with light hearts and renewed hope. The anxiety that once clouded their faces had lifted, replaced by confidence and a sense of direction, knowing that they were not alone on this journey.

Back in Guwahati, we planned a meeting with Dr. Bhutani. He interacted with the leaders with great warmth, respect and openness, assuring them of full support from the government, including access to schemes funded by World Bank. While his assurance was sincere and encouraging, it was also clear that the process would take time.

Meanwhile, Longki ji began the task of identifying and preparing a list of cadres who could first undergo the YLTP (Youth Leadership Training Program) at the Diphu Ashram, after which they would be sent to Bengaluru for further training. However, this step was met with significant resistance from the cadres themselves.

Many of them were reluctant to participate, having already attended multiple government-led training programs in the past. They carried a preconceived notion that this would be just another routine initiative—promising much but delivering little. Convincing them required patience, trust-building, and reassurance that this training was fundamentally different, aimed not just at skills, but at inner transformation and leadership rooted in responsibility and peace.

A batch of around 20 cadres, known to be among the most rebellious and drawn from six different organizations, arrived at the Diphu Ashram, largely out of compulsion, to begin the YLTP program. It was one of the most challenging batches we had ever handled, with high resistance and even higher expectations.

Yet, eight days of rigorous training worked its quiet magic. A deep inner shift took place. Resistance softened, trust emerged, and clarity replaced confusion. By the end of the program, they were ready, mentally and emotionally, to travel to Bengaluru, 3,230 kilometers away, a first such travel for many of them.

Logistically, the journey itself became a test of faith. There is only one weekly direct train from Diphu to Bengaluru, and securing tickets is almost impossible. I reached out to Deepak Choudhary ji, an IRS Officer, who assured me that confirmation would come, if at all, only at the very last moment.

Our first attempt ended in disappointment when the tickets were not confirmed. Undeterred, I booked tickets again for the following week. This time, just as hope was building, the train was cancelled due to floods in central India. Still, Deepak urged me to try once more, asking me to stay firm in faith.

With that trust, I tried booking tickets again, for the third week. Unfortunately, that too did not work out, as all seats were allotted under a minister's quota.

Despite repeated setbacks, the collective resolve remained unbroken. What was unfolding was not merely a logistical struggle—but a deeper test of patience, surrender, and faith that something far greater was guiding the journey.

Every Thursday, fifteen cadres would pack their belongings and wait at the Diphu Ashram, ready to board the train to Bengaluru. We repeated this process for three consecutive weeks. The last-minute cancellation of tickets created confusion, disappointment, and growing trust issues. Gradually, the cadres began to feel that they were being misled.

Their emotional turmoil was understandable. They were highly sensitive at this stage, and logic alone was no longer working. Nothing we said could ease their frustration or restore their confidence.

I discussed the situation again with Deepak ji, who reassured me that the tickets would be confirmed the following week. However, after three consecutive failures, even his confidence was shaken.

The fourth week came up, and I found myself wondering whether the cadres would even turn up.

At that moment, I clearly recollected Gurudev's instruction: "Bring them to the Bengaluru Ashram."

Without further delay or hesitation, I took the decisive step and booked flight tickets for them.

They finally reached Bengaluru, with a mix of excitement and quiet fear, uncertain of what lay ahead, yet ready to step into a new chapter of their lives.

The coordinators were briefed on their background, and I humbly requested that they overlook any initial mistakes, keeping the larger cause in mind. With time, the cadres began to settle in. They started attending the sessions regularly and took up solar light installation training with visible enthusiasm and sincerity.

When I arrived in Bengaluru, they approached me with a simple and heartfelt request; they expressed that they wanted to meet Gurudev.

It was clear that their inner journey had deepened. What had begun as a skill-training program was now evolving into something far more meaningful…a search for guidance, reassurance, and a deeper connection with the source that had inspired their transformation.

I took an appointment, and during the meeting, Tenzing Terang offered a Karbi *Poho*—a sacred symbol of the highest reverence and grace—to Gurudev. Gurudev enquired warmly about their well-being, and the interaction that followed became a once-in-a-lifetime experience for them.

Tenzing's first personal encounter with Gurudev at Bengaluru Ashram.

Simply being in Gurudev's presence worked wonders. Their doubts dissolved, complaints faded away, and the heaviness they carried for months lifted effortlessly. They left the meeting with renewed confidence, clarity and enthusiasm, deeply reassured that they were being guided and supported.

Thereafter, Tenzing began working with remarkable dedication. He went beyond classroom learning, deepened his *sadhana,* and took responsibility for motivating his group to envision and initiate something of their own. Gradually, he developed a clear understanding and began thinking from a larger, more inclusive perspective, moving from survival to leadership and long-term contribution.

After eight weeks of training, they all returned home as transformed individuals. Among them, Tenzing stood out for his extraordinary dedication. Using the skills he had acquired, he worked diligently, saved money, and independently took a flight back to Bengaluru to undergo advanced-level solar installation training.

A few months later, Tenzing called to share the news that he had successfully completed the next level of training. I was truly delighted to hear this. Not long after, he called again... this time, it was to inform me that he and his team had begun setting up solar projects in Mizoram and Meghalaya. It was nothing short of remarkable.

A few weeks later, Tenzing visited our Diphu Ashram. There was a deep reverence and quiet confidence in his eyes as he shared stories of installing solar lighting in remote and challenging regions across the Northeast, stretching from Arunachal Pradesh to Sikkim.

He was no longer burdened by uncertainty. He was content, purposeful, fully engaged, and genuinely happy—a living example of how inner transformation, combined with the right skills and guidance, can illuminate not just lives, but entire regions.

I witnessed a remarkable transformation in him ... from guns to social projects, from extortion to entrepreneurship. And it was not just Tenzing; his entire team began working day and night, creating livelihoods and offering direction to many youths who had once felt lost.

As he was about to leave, Tenzing quietly handed me an envelope. With a touch of shyness, he said, "Please keep this for the building of the Diphu Ashram."

Inside was ₹1,000—a small amount in monetary value, infinite in meaning.

It was a token of love, grace, and deep gratitude. I accepted it with a lump in my throat, overwhelmed by the journey it represented.

From guns to social projects, from extortion to entrepreneurship—this was not just Tenzing's journey, but a collective awakening. Today, KERUF sustains itself through farming, faith, and Gurudev's unconditional support. They often ask, with childlike longing, "When will Gurudev come to Karbi Anglong?"

This is a living testament to transformation, where conflict turns into contribution, fear into purpose, and despair into hope. Gurudev's *sankalpa* continues to ripple across regions: Kashmir to the Northeast, reminding us that peace is not an idea ... it is a lived reality.

And this is only the beginning.

15

The Divine Intervention

From guns and grenades to garlands and gamchas.

Once Gurudev gave his consent to be the interlocutor, we all returned with renewed hope and clarity. Gurudev then asked that the revised Charter of Demands be formally shared with the governor and chief minister of Assam, and with the Ministry of Home Affairs.

Accordingly, Etika ji and Mukteshwar ji submitted the revised demands to the government, clearly stating that the group wished to have Gurudev as the Interlocutor in their dialogue with the Indian authorities.

Having Gurudev by their side added immense weight to their Charter of Demands and brought a deep sense of sincerity to the entire process. Anyone who read the document could immediately sense the values, integrity and grace that Gurudev embodies. Moreover, Gurudev had also suggested that they meet the honorable chief minister in person.

Etika ji and Mukteshwar ji sent letters to all the concerned authorities and began seeking appointments with the ministers. However, despite repeated efforts, nothing seemed to move forward. For nearly four months, they ran from pillar to post, yet no one showed any real interest in meeting them.

I, too, followed up continuously, but the situation remained completely stagnant; nothing was moving at all.

Every time I interacted with them, they would gently but firmly remind me, "Gurudev is our Interlocutor."

So, on 13th April 2023, though I had no idea what Gurudev might have done behind the scenes, I received a message from Prashant Nair ji asking, "Do you have any updates on the DNLA group?"

I informed him that they were still running from pillar to post, struggling to get an appointment with the honorable chief minister of Assam. Prashant ji conveyed this update to Gurudev.

There was a brief pause.

Gurudev then calmly assured that everything would come to a logical conclusion. In that stillness, something shifted. There was something profoundly divine in his words, an unshakable calm that dissolved all doubt and quietly reaffirmed faith.

On 19th April 2023, to everyone's astonishment, they were finally received by Chief Minister Shri Himanta Biswa Sarma, at his official residence. The setting itself spoke of authority and gravity, yet what stood out most was the warmth of the moment. In the photographs captured then, the chief minister was holding their hands firmly…an unmistakable gesture of reassurance and trust.

Their faces told a deeper story. The years of uncertainty seemed to soften, replaced by a quiet confidence and a visible spark in their eyes. Watching those images, I felt a deep inner knowing: the silent magic of Gurudev was already in motion.

They presented their Charter of Demands, clearly stating their heartfelt wish for Gurudev to be their interlocutor. The chief minister listened attentively and was made fully aware of Gurudev's sincere intention and commitment to guide the process toward peace, dialogue and a lasting resolution.

Ideally, a formal surrender process takes a couple of months. However, in this case, there was a divine acceleration.

The entire governmental process was personally monitored by the chief minister, ensuring that nothing was delayed.

To everyone's amazement, within just one week, on 27 April 2023, they travelled to Delhi and signed a Memorandum of Settlement—a historic tripartite agreement between the Government of Assam, the Government of India, and the DNLA. This moment marked the end of decades of violence in Dima Hasao district, Karbi Anglong district, Hojai, and few other red zones in Assam.

Most significantly, the DNLA was the last active militant group in Assam, bringing a long and painful chapter in the state's history to a peaceful and hopeful close.

A total of 181 cadres of the Dimasa National Liberation Army (DNLA), along with two hundred civil members of Dimasa People's Supreme Council laid down their arms in the presence of the Hon'ble Chief Minister Shri Himanta Biswa Sarma and his cabinet members on 29 October 2023 at Nityalal Daolaguphu Sports Stadium Ground, Haflong in Dima Hasao district of Assam, and formally returned to the mainstream, as reported by *India Today NE*.

Along with the surrender of arms, each former DNLA cadre was provided a one-time financial assistance in the form of a fixed deposit of INR 4,00,000, as part of the government's rehabilitation package. This support was aimed at helping them rebuild their lives and reintegrate into society with dignity and stability.

In his statement, Chief Minister Himanta Biswa Sarma described the surrender as a "historic day" for Assam and for the nation. He reaffirmed the government's commitment to the development and well-being of the Dimasa people and assured that all necessary assistance would be extended to the surrendered cadres to ensure their smooth transition into a peaceful and productive life.

On 27 April 2023, the hon'ble chief minister of Assam, Dr. Himanta Biswa Sarma, quoted Gurudev's tweet and expressed his gratitude, saying:

"Jai Gurudev!

Gratitude for all your efforts in bringing peace to Assam. Through compassion and dialogue, you have inspired peace and the motivation for resolution. May this divine work continue to grow and guide us eternally."

Subsequently, on 29 April 2023, the Hon'ble Member of Parliament Shri Horen Sing Bey also acknowledged Gurudev's role and tweeted:

"Thank you, Gurudev. It is because of your continued support and guidance that the DNLA has successfully signed the peace accord with the Government of Assam and the Government of India. This accord will further restore peace, prosperity, and development in the region."

Inspired by Gurudev, the DNLA created a historic milestone, moving from militancy to the mainstream. This transformation was possible only through Gurudev's *sankalpa,* his vision of a stress-free and violence-free society.

A few days later, I received a call from Etika. He wished to meet Gurudev in person and express his heartfelt gratitude. As he spoke, the memories of the many *mental sandwich* moments flashed through my mind; yet everything now felt clear, complete, and inevitable.

We booked the tickets.

When Gurudev saw them, there was an exchange of pure, wordless bliss. Their eyes reflected surrender and relief; Gurudev's presence radiated reassurance and grace. They requested a photograph, and Gurudev, with his gentle smile, invited them instead to come and sit in the *satsang*.

In that simple invitation, the journey, from guns to grace, found its quiet fulfillment.

That evening's *satsang* was attended by nearly 20,000 people and was live telecast across the world. Gurudev invited us onto the stage and asked me to introduce them to the gathering.

Gurudev blessing Etika and Mukteshwar at Bengaluru Ashram.

After the introduction, Mukteshwar ji took the microphone. With folded hands, he said, *"Jai Gurudev,"* and began sharing his feelings and the blessings he had received from Gurudev... in simple, broken English, yet spoken straight from the heart. As he spoke, the entire venue fell into pin-drop silence. Every word carried the weight of transformation.

He then presented an appreciation note to Gurudev. His voice trembled, choked with emotion. Etika stood beside him, overwhelmed, just unable to speak.

When they completed their expression of gratitude, the silence gave way to a thunderous applause. It was not merely an applause; it was the victory of peace, the fulfillment of Gurudev's *sankalpa,* a living testimony to divine intervention.

Gurudev gently showered them with lotus petals, blessed them, and enquired about their well-being. Then, with infinite compassion, he said: "This is your home. You can always come here."

In that moment, the journey was complete... from violence to surrender, from fear to belonging, from the margins to the very heart.

I was filled with deep gratitude as I witnessed this extraordinary transformation. We were scheduled to return to Assam the very next day. As it turned out, I was travelling back with them, and unfortunately, we had mistakenly booked a flight for a date one month later. We quickly corrected the error and booked the next available flight, which left us with ample time together at the airport.

It was during this waiting period that I received an unexpected call. The person on the other end remarked that *whatever we had done did not make any sense*. The comment hit me hard. I was utterly shocked. Years of sincere effort and silent perseverance were suddenly dismissed by a few careless words.

In that moment, I felt a surge of anger and deep hurt; conflicting emotions rising together, unsettling the peace I had been carrying.

Sensing the turbulence in my mind, Etika gently turned to me and said, "Vishnu ji, you know, when Gurudev was showering rose petals on us during the *satsang,* we felt as though Gurudev had erased the karmas of many lifetimes at once. How blessed you are, Gurudev has chosen you to do his work."

Aha!

In that instant, a deep wave of relief washed over me. I realized how a single careless comment had momentarily disturbed my state of mind, and how unnecessary it truly was. Here was Etika, who had walked the path from conflict to surrender, now playing the role of a guru to me, lifting my inner state with such simplicity and wisdom.

I stood stunned and deeply moved. Once again, I witnessed how Gurudev works ... not always directly, but through people, through moments, through grace, to elevate our consciousness.

It was, unmistakably, divine intervention in action.

If anything, the episode helped me drop any *'doership'* that I was carrying.

From guns and grenades to garlands and gamchas, from fear to grace and gratitude, Gurudev has been constantly guiding and protecting us. Through him, divinity radiates as peace, compassion, and profound transformation. What unfolded was not merely a political process, but a divine intervention in its truest sense.

The peace agreement has ushered in a remarkable transformation across the region. Roads and infrastructure have improved, medical facilities have expanded, and for the first time, many from the region have successfully entered government services. In a moment of deep pride and healing, the Dimasa people hosted a cabinet meeting of the Government of Assam in their own region, and notably, a cabinet minister today hails from the same land once marked by conflict.

This journey—from violence to belonging, from resistance to responsibility—stands as a living testament to the power of dialogue, compassion, and Gurudev's *sankalpa* for a peaceful and harmonious society.

Etika, Mukteshwar, and their team continue to work tirelessly, overseeing the development and well-being of their region. This is just the beginning of the beautiful world we all aspire to create together.

DNLA team expressing their gratitude to Gurudev.

With the last and final group returning to the mainstream, Assam today stands more peaceful than it has been in decades. Yet the journey continues, guided by the eternal light of the Master. We shall not hang up our boots until the last gun in the region is laid down, choosing peace over conflict, and compassion over fear.

16

Peace in Manipur

A quiet turning point!

Gurudev Sri Sri Ravi Shankar ji spoke the line "We will not stop until the last gun is laid down in this region" during the Strength in Diversity: North East Indigenous People's Conference, which was held in Guwahati, Assam on 7 September 2017. This was part of his keynote address at the historic peace conference focused on dialogue, reconciliation and ending decades of conflict in the Northeast of India.

To my knowledge, Gurudev has been working tirelessly for many years to bring peace to the Northeast. His silent *sankalpa*, boundless compassion, and inclusive vision have touched countless lives … far beyond what is visible to the eye.

Among our senior devotees was someone whose own life reflected this transformation. He had once been a militant, but through Gurudev's guidance, he underwent a profound inner change and later became an Art of Living teacher. His journey stood as a living testimony to the power of inner transformation. Despite his past, or perhaps because of it, he carried immense humility and depth. He always treated me with great love and respect.

One day, he called me. There was a certain earnestness in his voice. He said he needed my help, to meet someone and inspire him to come and meet Gurudev.

Initially, I was reluctant. I knew this devotee still had connections from his underground days, even though he had completely and joyfully transitioned into a normal, dignified life. Yet, he kept insisting that I must meet this person in Manipur. His conviction was unwavering, rooted not in fear or force, but in faith...faith that a single meeting with Gurudev could change the course of a life, just as it had changed his.

Looking back, I realize that these are not isolated incidents, but part of a much larger movement, where guns are replaced by wisdom, violence by surrender, and fear by trust. And this journey of peace has only just begun.

After numerous requests, he finally revealed why he was so insistent. He told me that he wanted me to meet the chief of the United National Liberation Front (UNLF), Manipur.

I asked him plainly, *"Whom do you want me to meet?"*

He replied calmly, "R.K. Meghen." Then he asked me to search his name on Google.

A quick search revealed that R.K. Meghen was the founder of the UNLF, a militant organization demanding a separate Manipur. Known as *Sana Yaima,* Rajkumar Meghen had been charged by the National Investigation Agency (NIA) for "waging war" against India. He had spent nearly ten years in prison.

My Art of Living friend then shared something even more striking. Long back, Gurudev himself had once gone to meet R.K. Meghen in jail. However, at that time, R.K. Meghen was extremely reluctant and did not wish to meet him.

Listening to all this, I understood the gravity of what was being asked of me. This was not a casual meeting, nor an ordinary request—it was an invitation into a space where years of conflict, resistance, and mistrust existed, and where only compassion and grace could open a door.

R.K. Meghen reportedly joined the United National Liberation Front (UNLF) in 1976. A year earlier, in 1975, he had left Manipur and undertaken a difficult trek to a militant camp in Myanmar's Somra Tract, which at the time was led by Thuingaleng Muivah and S. S. Khaplang. Notably, his younger son was only six days old when he left home.

Over the years, Meghen rose steadily through the ranks and became the chairman of the UNLF in 1998.

In 2010, he was arrested in Bangladesh and subsequently handed over to Indian authorities. The National Investigation Agency (NIA) charged him, along with 18 other leaders, with waging war against India and raising funds through extortion from state government departments and private entities.

In June 2016, a special NIA court convicted him under multiple sections of the Indian Penal Code and the Unlawful Activities (Prevention) Act, sentencing him to ten years' imprisonment. Meghen declined to seek leniency and rejected the authority of Indian courts to try him.

During his incarceration at Guwahati Central Jail, he reportedly made constructive contributions to prison life by helping establish a library, starting a music program for inmates, and assisting in the creation of a garden within the jail premises. In November 2019, his sentence was reduced by approximately ten months in recognition of these efforts.

He was released from prison amid what was widely perceived as a strategic move in the broader context of the ongoing peace negotiations in the region. However, following his release, the NIA initially disallowed him from returning immediately to Manipur. He was instead moved to a safe house in Guwahati and later to Delhi. On 28 November, he was finally permitted to travel to Imphal.

Since then, R.K. Meghen has lived a quiet life, largely away from public view and media attention.

Considering the gravity of the situation, and guided by an inner confidence that something good was awaiting, I first checked with Karthik ji, Gurudev's secretary. He responded with a clear go-ahead. With that assurance, I booked my tickets, and we left for Manipur.

I stayed at our Art of Living center in Imphal—a place that truly feels like home. I was warmly received by Rajaque ji and Brahmachari Premswarup ji. Our loving devotees from Manipur welcomed us with abundant local food and, more importantly, immense affection and care.

The next morning, we were scheduled to meet R.K. Meghen, who at that time was under house arrest as per government directives.

We met R.K. Meghen and I offered him Gurudev's shawl, along with the book *Celebrating Silence.* He received us with visible joy and warmth. He was living peacefully with his wife and soon began sharing his experiences from the past five decades; stories shaped by struggle, conviction, and deep contemplation.

He was soft-spoken, yet his presence naturally evoked reverence and respect. What struck me most was his remarkable command over international relations and geopolitical thought. I listened patiently, without judgment, occasionally asking questions, allowing the conversation to unfold naturally.

At a certain point, I gently asked him whether he would like to meet Gurudev in person.

He responded with a clear yes, expressing that he would like a formal invitation to visit Bengaluru. He was genuinely happy that we had come to meet him and, with great humility, invited us to join him for dinner at his home.

Without a second thought, I agreed. It felt like a blessing; an opportunity to spend more time with him, to listen more deeply, and to witness how silence, sincerity, and grace can quietly soften even the most hardened chapters of life.

I returned to our Art of Living center and immediately connected with Karthik ji regarding the invitation. By evening, we received confirmation: an invitation for R.K. Meghen to meet Gurudev.

We then went back to his residence and shared a lovely vegetarian dinner together. It truly felt like being with family; the love and warmth we received were unmatched. There was no formality, only simplicity, openness, and mutual respect.

R.K. Meghen continued sharing his life stories—his challenges, reflections, and possible solutions, drawing from his decades of experience. He spoke at length about the Kukis and the Meiteis, shedding light on the deeper roots of the conflict and offering thoughtful perspectives on what could be done to bring lasting and permanent peace to Manipur.

As I listened, it became clear to me that when dialogue is rooted in sincerity and silence, even the most complex conflicts begin to reveal pathways toward understanding.

The Meitei–Kuki conflict in Manipur, which erupted in May 2023, is a complex ethnic and political crisis rooted in historical tensions, land rights, identity, and governance. At its core lies a deep divide between the Imphal Valley and the surrounding hill areas, inhabited predominantly by different ethnic communities with distinct constitutional protections and social realities.

The Meitei community, which forms the majority population and largely resides in the Imphal Valley, has long demanded Scheduled Tribe (ST) status. They argue that such recognition is necessary to protect their culture, land, and identity. However, the Kuki-Zo and other hill tribal communities strongly oppose this demand, fearing that granting ST status to the Meiteis would dilute existing constitutional safeguards meant specifically for hill tribes, particularly regarding land ownership and political representation.

The immediate trigger for the violence was a judicial development. On 14 April 2023, the Manipur High Court passed an order that appeared to recommend consideration of Scheduled Tribe status for the Meitei community. This order was later criticized by the Supreme Court. In response, on 3 May 2023, tribal groups organized protest rallies against the Meitei demand, while Meitei groups held counter-rallies and blockades. Following one such rally, clashes broke out near the border areas of Churachandpur and Bishnupur districts, quickly escalating into widespread violence, including arson and retaliatory attacks.

According to government figures, as of 22 November 2024, the violence has resulted in the deaths of at least 258 people and the displacement of nearly 60,000 individuals. Thousands have been injured, dozens remain missing, and extensive destruction has occurred—over 4,700 houses have been burnt and hundreds of religious structures, including temples and churches have been vandalized. Unofficial estimates suggest the actual toll may be significantly higher.

Beyond the immediate trigger, the conflict is also intertwined with longstanding issues such as uneven development between the valley and hill regions, mistrust between communities, concerns over illegal drug trade and poppy cultivation in hill areas, and perceptions of administrative bias or inaction. Together, these factors have deepened ethnic polarisation and made reconciliation increasingly difficult.

The crisis in Manipur underscores the urgent need for dialogue, trust-building, and inclusive peace efforts that go beyond political solutions—efforts rooted in empathy, dignity, and a shared vision for coexistence.

I carefully redirected the conversation toward practical next steps and requested him to confirm his travel dates to Bengaluru. We exchanged phone numbers, and soon after, I returned to the Diphu Ashram.

That journey left a deep imprint on me. I felt, more than ever, that Gurudev's compassion has no limits. In that experience, I sensed that the same compassion was flowing through me as well. I felt deeply loved and cared for, and I could also see a subtle spark of love and trust awakening in R.K. Meghen.

Within a few days, he confirmed his travel plans. He would be coming to Bengaluru with his wife and team. When they arrived, I felt immense joy and gratitude as I welcomed them at the Bengaluru airport.

It was a moment that words can scarcely capture: a former militant leader from Manipur, who had led the UNLF for decades, now arriving with a quiet longing for peace, seeking solace in the presence of Gurudev.

In that moment, it became clear to me once again: when compassion is unconditional and silence is sincere, even the longest journeys of conflict can gently turn toward peace.

At the age of 78, R.K. Meghen arrived at our Bengaluru Ashram and was visibly amazed by the diversity of people present there. On introducing him to a few strangers at the ashram, they warmly spoke about polo, the sport closely associated with Manipur, and praised the natural beauty and rich culture of the state. R.K. Meghen was taken by surprise and deeply moved, wondering how people from so many different parts of the world knew and appreciated Manipur.

What left an even deeper impression on him was seeing seekers from across the globe coming to Gurudev, each looking for their own personal space of peace, clarity and belonging.

When our meeting was scheduled, Gurudev welcomed R.K. Meghen and his family with a shawl. They, in turn, offered several traditional gifts to Gurudev, which he received graciously. The atmosphere was filled with warmth, dignity, and mutual respect.

Gurudev listened attentively as R.K. Meghen shared his thoughts and experiences. They discussed in detail the prevailing situation in Manipur, particularly the ongoing conflict between the Meitei and the Kuki communities. Gurudev's listening was deep and compassionate—creating a space where decades of pain, struggle, and aspiration could be spoken without fear or resistance.

It was a moment where dialogue transcended politics and entered the realm of healing.

Gurudev shared that both these communities have coexisted for generations, and that the present situation is a testing phase. He emphasized the need for patience and perseverance, acknowledging that deep wounds take time to heal and that lasting peace cannot be rushed.

The interaction was deeply practical and grounded. Gurudev's understanding of current affairs and his clarity in offering realistic, workable perspectives went far beyond ordinary comprehension. His guidance was neither ideological nor emotional—it was rooted in wisdom, experience, and compassion.

R.K. Meghen with Gurudev at Bengaluru Ashram.

R.K. Meghen had a truly heartfelt experience during the interaction. He later submitted a memorandum to Gurudev, which Gurudev received and kept with great care. In that moment, a long-held resistance seemed to gently dissolve, making space for grace, trust, and guidance.

Later, Bhanumaa spent time with R.K. Meghen and his family. They felt deeply loved, cared for, and genuinely heard. They expressed immense gratitude for the opportunity to be in the presence of the Master.

R.K. Meghen with Bhanumaa at Bengaluru Ashram

What unfolded was not merely a meeting; it was a quiet moment of healing, where dialogue met silence, and conflict began its subtle journey toward peace.

Later, a group representing Meitei organizations came to meet Gurudev. He listened to them attentively and gently advised them to remain patient during these challenging times, reminding them that restraint and dialogue are essential for lasting peace.

Subsequently, a third group met Gurudev and submitted a memorandum seeking guidance and support for restoring peace in Manipur. Gurudev received their concerns with equal openness and compassion.

Manipuri group meeting Gurudev.

Through these interactions—and many others that remain unseen—Gurudev has been working both directly and indirectly to bring peace to Manipur. His approach has always been inclusive, impartial, and rooted in dialogue, patience, and inner transformation.

Often, the most powerful peace efforts unfold quietly, without publicity. What matters is that hearts begin to soften, conversations begin to open, and hope slowly finds its way back into a land that has known too much suffering.

While I was writing this book, I received a call from Bhushan ji, Gurudev's secretary, based in the USA. At that time, I was conducting Sahaj Meditation initiations. After the session, I noticed a couple of missed calls from him.

A protest was underway in Karbi Anglong, and Gurudev—who was in Canada at the time—wanted to personally ensure that all of us were safe and well. Later, during a video call, Gurudev shared something that left a deep impression on me. He said that we must continue striving for peace, especially in the Northeast.

This understanding goes far beyond my comprehension. To see the world through the Master's eyes—to witness such constant awareness, care, and responsibility for every corner of the land—is a truly divine experience.

In moments like these, I realize that peace is not just an action or an event; it is a continuous state of concern, compassion, and commitment. And to walk even a small part of that path is, in itself, *a blessing.*

A group of participants from Manipur came to our Diphu Ashram and graduated from the *Blessing Program.* When they returned home, they began sharing their own experiences, of healing people and touching hearts. Many spoke of changes that felt almost miraculous. This was soft power at work, a subtle and gentle touch. In quiet ways, Gurudev continues to heal society there.

What deeply shapes my perception of Gurudev is his sensitivity to even the smallest pain felt by those who are suffering, and his constant awareness of what can best be done to heal them. His compassion is not momentary; it is continuous and all-embracing.

Love, I have realized, is not merely an emotion; it is our very existence.

The peace process, too, is ongoing. Yet I hold unwavering faith that Gurudev's vision and his *sankalpa* will manifest fully—as a peaceful, stress-free, and violence-free society in Manipur and across the entire Northeast.

There is a deep and abiding gratitude in being chosen by the Master—to be shaped as his instrument and guided by his wisdom, love, and blessings. This grace brings with it not pride, but responsibility: the responsibility to serve, to listen, and to act with compassion. Inspired by Gurudev's vision, we remain committed to nurturing a society free from stress and violence, where dialogue replaces division, understanding dissolves fear, and love becomes a lived reality. With faith in his *sankalpa* and patience in the process, we walk forward, knowing that when intention is pure and service is sincere, peace is not distant; it is inevitable.

Epilogue: When will Gurudev Come?

Waiting is also a form of preparation…

A Guru never takes any *sankalpa*; He is free.

The disciples take the *sankalpa* and carry it out with the blessings of the Master.

The Guru is pure, full, and complete, and leads the way towards realizing the Highest.

One day, we had an appointment with Gurudev. I had brought a map of the Northeast with me. Before I could even ask him anything, He said, "You want to ask when Gurudev will be coming to Karbi Anglong."

I laughed with pure joy, realizing that Gurudev already knew what was in my mind.

Immediately, I proposed to Gurudev that we wanted to build a *kutir* for him at our Diphu Ashram. Gurudev, in his compassion, shared that he would manage. But I insisted, "No, Gurudev, we need to have a *kutir*."

Again, with great compassion, Gurudev said it was alright. Yet, with deep humility, I submitted once more that it was important for us to have Gurudev's *kutir* in our ashram. Finally, with all his compassion, Gurudev agreed and said, "Okay, make a small one with bamboo—10 by 15 feet."

It was clear guidance on the project.

I returned full of enthusiasm and worked with an architect to prepare a drawing, which was later approved by Gurudev's secretariat. The project was very dear to me because, once completed, we would have the opportunity to host Gurudev.

When Covid arrived, I received an email from our Bengaluru team asking us to stop the work immediately. I wanted clarification, as we had already raised funds and issued a work order, but no one responded with any clear explanation.

I then felt guided to check directly with Gurudev and sent him a message. Gurudev replied,

"No need of my *kutir* now."

While reading the message, I actually fainted. All my dreams of bringing Gurudev felt shattered. I was in deep pain, and my sense of purpose seemed to come to a halt. Caught in a storm of emotions, I could neither eat nor sleep. I kept rereading the message: "No need of my *kutir* now."

I called Maaji and shared my mental restlessness with her. She asked me to read the message again: "No need of my *kutir* now."

Then she said gently, "You are just a fool… no need of my *kutir* now."

At that moment, I realized what I had been missing—the now.

My mind had stopped comprehending because I was overlooking the greatness of the *now* in Gurudev's message. Aha! I felt completely relaxed. Maaji explained that during Covid, no one could travel, and the funds were needed for development and social activities rather than construction. Gurudev had clearly said that at this time, a *kutir* was not needed—but he never said that he would not come.

I was overjoyed and began laughing at my small mind, which had been miserable for almost ten days.

Every few hours, I would call Maaji, and she would gently ask me to read the message once again. It took me a week to return to normal.

Many times, we devotees do not truly listen and instead jump to conclusions midway.

Gurudev says, "The Art of Living starts with the art of listening—listening to what is being said, not what you want to hear."

My prayers remained intact, and I gained renewed confidence to work harder, with greater faith and prayerfulness.

Sangeeta Jani ji, a revered Art of Living faculty member and an old-timer with Gurudev, once visited the Diphu Ashram to conduct a Silence Retreat.

Her presence itself carried a depth of stillness. After guiding participants through profound silence and meditation, she conducted a beautiful Guru Pooja, invoking grace, gratitude, and the living presence of the Master.

On that sacred occasion, she inaugurated Gurudev's temple in our Vaikuntha Hall. It was not merely a ritual… it felt like consecration, as if the space had been waiting for that very moment.

With deep faith and quiet certainty, she said, "The Divine will come one day."

Those words settled into our hearts like a blessing…a sankalpa offered into time. Since then, they continue to echo within us; reminding us to serve, to wait, and to trust in his divine timing.

Eventually, Gurudev approved the completion of the *kutir* after Covid. The work began again with full enthusiasm and was completed with a unique blend of traditional and modern design, facing Jambili Athon, the traditional Karbi totem.

When we showed Gurudev that the *kutir* was complete, even he looked at it with wonder.

Now, every time I take guests to the Bengaluru Ashram, I begin to ask, "Gurudev, when are you coming to—"

Before I can finish, Gurudev fills in the blank,"Karbi Anglong."

And we both laugh.

To my surprise, once when we had a group of ministers visiting, Gurudev began the conversation by saying, "Vishnu keeps asking me to come to Karbi Anglong."

The chief executive member of Karbi Anglong Autonomous Council, Dr. Tuliram Ronghan, Sh. Horen Sing Bey, Member of Parliament and the entire council personally invited Gurudev to visit Karbi Anglong.

We also had many devotees who would humbly meet Gurudev and ask, "Gurudev, when will you be coming to Karbi Anglong?"

Devotees inviting Gurudev to Karbi Anglong.

Gurudev sent his secretary a couple of times for higher-level programs. One day, during a call with Gurudev, I shared, "Gurudev, before Shivji comes, Nandi visits," pointing to his secretary. Gurudev laughed heartily.

We all said, "We are waiting for you in Karbi Anglong." Gurudev paused for a moment and said, "Okay, Vishnu."

Over time, I noticed that in all my meetings, I would have only this one question in my mind—and Gurudev would affirm it with a "yes" every time. Gradually, I realized there was no need to keep asking the same question repeatedly. So one day, I decided not to bring it up again.

In the *darshan* line, surrounded by so many devotees, Gurudev looked at me and began enquiring, "How is everyone there? How is the weather? Is everyone happy? Blessings for all."

Devotees Inviting Gurudev to Diphu Ashram.

The next time, when I had decided not to ask, Gurudev said, "Vishnu, you prepare, and I will come."

So, every time I interacted with Gurudev, the topic of visiting Karbi Anglong would somehow come up.

One fine day, Gurudev's secretariat called me and immediately asked me to send the location of the Diphu Ashram. Later, I realized that Gurudev wanted to stop by personally, but it was not logistically practical considering his travel schedule.

Our special friends have also invited Gurudev many times whenever they met him. They feel that militancy will disappear forever the moment Gurudev's feet touch the land of Karbi Anglong.

Devotees inviting Gurudev to Northeast.

On one occasion, a group of devotees officially went to invite Gurudev. He met everyone, and all fifty people personally expressed their desire in a queue, saying, "Gurudev, we are waiting for you in Karbi Anglong."

Gurudev looked into each person's eyes and nodded, and every devotee left feeling joyful and blessed.

Gurudev invited by a team to inaugurate Diphu Ashram.

Later that same evening, we had a *satsang* at Vishalakshi Mantap. We were filled with happiness and bliss from meeting Gurudev. During the *satsang*, unexpectedly and beyond our imagination, Gurudev shared, "We have so many devotees from Karbi Anglong. You know, we have a very beautiful ashram there."

Though he did not explicitly say, "I will be coming soon," all of us felt it deeply in our hearts.

During the World Cultural Festival 2023 in Washington DC, Gurudev personally enquired about everyone's well-being and also asked about the devotees in the Northeast.

Later, Gurudev blessed me as a *Kaal Gyani*. Many people ask me, "When is Gurudev coming to Diphu?

I simply smile, pray, and ask them to intensify their prayers. I have no answers—only gratitude.

Devotees inviting Gurudev to North East.

One day, a devotee, Dr Sanghmitra Bose, came to the ashram and wished to make a donation. After doing so, she asked me to show her Gurudev's *kutir*, which at that time had only six pillars.

I have a habit of doing Yoga Nidra after lunch, so I told her, "Why don't you go ahead, and I will join you later?"

She returned and shared that she had experienced Gurudev's *darshan* at the *kutir*. I was amazed—she could feel his presence. It reminded me of the story of Rishi Matang, where Shabari took Lord Rama to the place where Rishi Matang used to meditate, and Rama could feel the divine presence of the rishi.

Devotion has the power to make anyone feel the presence of Gurudev. Though Gurudev has never personally visited, we have all felt his constant presence time and again. With each program and meditation, we deepen our *sankalpa* to host Gurudev in his own ashram.

A Master has ways that are often unfathomable. Perhaps we need to drop our restlessness and bring greater intensity to the mission we are working on. For Gurudev, in my personal understanding, it is not about a place—it is about the place he holds in the heart.

Every day, what gives me a spark is the thought: *"What if Gurudev is coming today—are we ready?"* This is the only driving force.

A few days ago, Krishna Sastry ji, Gurudev's secretary, during a *Sanyam* follow-up, shared with all of us, "Gurudev was enquiring about the Diphu Ashram, and he also conveyed that everyone there wishes for his physical presence."

Our prayers are always heard and answered; it is only a matter of time. The Divine will fulfil this wish, and the question will transform into a living wonder: *"Gurudev is in Diphu Ashram."*

Recently, Gurudev asked me, "Vishnu, all good?"

I shared, "Gurudev, we are all waiting for you at—"

And before I could finish, Gurudev, with his most mischievous smile, filled in the blank:

"Karbi Anglong."

Gurudev enquiring about the Northeast.

Once again, Prof. Ashok Puranik (Director at AIIMS Guwahati) met Gurudev Sri Sri Ravi Shankar and extended an invitation to visit the Northeast.

Gurudev looked into my eyes and said, *"Diphu has been long due."*

It went straight to my heart. In that moment, I felt... Gurudev knows what silently keeps running in my mind, what I hold close in my prayers.

Such simple gestures are profound reminders...that we only need to wait, trust, and pray. Everything unfolds at the right time, through his grace.

As I write these words, the prayer is alive in the heart, and the wishes of thousands will be fulfilled very soon. Gurudev will come, and it will become a historic moment.

Prof Puranik inviting Gurudev to the Northeast.

Wow, so wonderful
Is the love I am experiencing.
My heart expanding with compassion,
The mind amplifying imagination.
You have captured my heart with your love.

Wow, so wonderful
Is the love I am experiencing.
Every breath I breathe
Brings a smile with ease.
The intellect flourishes in intuition,
And life is blossoming with joy.
You have captured my heart with your love.

I am waiting… I am waiting…
No eyes have seen,
No ears have heard,
My heart truly knows.
Longing for you is full of love.

Within you, I lose myself.
With You, I find myself.
I want to lose again,
Though you are in my heart.

Wow, so wonderful
Is the longing for you.
My eyes are looking for you...
Come soon...
Come soon...

AIN'T THAT A MIRACLE?: An Unlikely Journey Into Music and Meditation

Jeremy Occhipinti

979-8885751353

A moving, humorous memoir tracing Jeremy Occhipinti's journey through illness, music, teaching, and spiritual discovery under Gurudev Sri Sri Ravi Shankar—highlighting resilience, service, and the miracle of inner transformation.

THE MAN WHO FROZE FIRE: True Stories of Conflict Transformation by Sanjay Kumar Guided by Gurudev Sri Sri Ravi Shankar

Suraj Duseja

979-8885750707

This book shares true stories of conflict transformation from Bihar, Northeast, and Kashmir, showcasing how peace was built in violent zones under the grassroots leadership of Sanjay Kumar, guided by Gurudev Sri Sri Ravi Shankar.

SCIENTIFIC YOGI:

A Scientific Look at Yoga
A Spiritual Perspective on Science

Tulsi Arora

979-8885752763

This book bridges Vedic wisdom, Yogic practice, and modern science, exploring their shared quest for unity and evidence of convergence between inner and outer discovery.

MEETING WITH THE MASTERS

Rishi Taavi Kassila

978-1942426264

Taavi Kassila's spiritual journey spans interviews with global masters—Dalai Lama, Sai Baba, Krishnamurti—culminating with Amma. This compelling memoir offers rare insights into meditation, enlightenment, and the search for a true guru.

THE QUANTUM BOOK OF SOMA: Reinterpreting the Wisdom of the Vedas

Maj. Gen. G D Bakshi

978-1942426769

"This book examines Vedic Soma's botanical, biological, and philosophical essence, merging Rig Veda, Upanishads, and quantum physics to provide modern seekers deep metaphysical insights into consciousness and existence."

Time - Book 1: Kala Gati | The Cosmic Flow of Time and History

Ajay Chaturvedi

979-8885752268

Kāla Gati explores how cosmic Time shapes human history, blending Vedic insights with science, astronomy, and philosophy—revealing timeless wisdom from ancient India's calendars, consciousness studies, and enduring ecological traditions.